Cabela's®

WORLD'S FOREMOST OUTFITTER

A
HISTORY

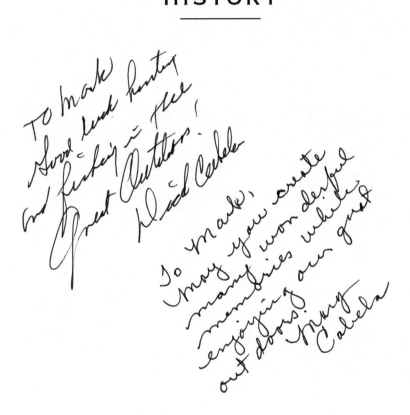

To mark
Good luck hunting
and fishing in the
Great Outdoors!
Dick Cabela

To mark,
may you create
many wonderful
memories while
enjoying our great
outdoors! Mary
Cabela

Cabela's ®
WORLD'S FOREMOST OUTFITTER ®
A HISTORY

DAVID CABELA

INTRODUCTION BY
CHUCK YEAGER
BRIGADIER GENERAL, USAF, RETIRED

Paul S. Eriksson, *Publisher*
Forest Dale, Vermont

© 2001 by David Cabela

Printed in the United States of America.

5 4 3 2 1

Library of Congress Cataloging-in-Publication Data

Cabela, David, 1972-
  Cabela's, world's foremost outfitters : a history / by David Cabela ; introduction by Chuck Yeager.
    p. cm.
  Includes index.
  ISBN 0-8397-1280-4
    1. Cabela's (Firm)--History. 2. Sporting goods industry--United States--History. 3. Camping equipment industry--United States--History. 4. Fishing equipment industry--United States--History. I. Cabela's (Firm) II. Title.

HD9992.U54C333 2001
388.7'6687'0941--dc21

2001033070

The poem, "The Guy in the Glass," by Dale Wimbrow (© 1934) is reprinted by permission of Peter Dale Wimbrow, Jr., son of the author.

Design by Eugenie S. Delaney

In loving memory of
A.C. and Marian Cabela and
Teresa Kerns

Contents

Photographs follow pages 44 and 148.

Preface

MOST OF US DREAM of achieving success. Whether those accomplishments be financial, spiritual or family prosperity, we all have our personal goals by which we measure our achievements. There are hundreds of ways we can measure our success, or for that matter the success of others.

One can argue that I may be biased, but two of the most successful people I have had the great pleasure to know are my parents, Dick and Mary Cabela.

By any standard, they have been formidable in business, building a world-renowned outdoor-outfitting company literally from scratch. But their achievements go much deeper than just financial prosperity. They are also accomplished parents. For as they worked very hard to build a dream, they also worked hard to build a strong faith and a family consisting of nine children who continually made their lives more difficult (I can personally attest to this).

Yet, through all the difficult times, they have also been victorious in a part of life that all too many people fail at these days. Through endless nights of trying to get their business off the ground, and with nine hair-raising children, they have been triumphant in marriage. The passion they share for the outdoors has played a significant role in allowing the love they feel for each other to grow.

One of the human species' earliest and greatest skills is the art of hunting. Hunting has undergone many changes over time, from an essential to basic survival to the recreational lifestyle it has largely become today. Women's role in hunting may be the most significant change of contemporary times. Not long ago, hunting and fishing were considered man-only fields of recreation, with few exceptions. Today, Dick *and* Mary Cabela share the aesthetic art of hunting together.

I have had the honor of sharing the hunt with my mother and father and believe that their love for animals and the outdoors has helped them gain the success that has encompassed every facet of their lives.

I hope this story will show, in even just a small way, that success does not come easily. It takes the hard work, cooperation and dedication that Dick, Mary, and Jim Cabela believed in and practiced for so much to be achieved. It is a factual account of how a dream went from the kitchen table to the World's Foremost Outfitter, but at times it comes from the perspective of a son and a nephew who witnessed much of this success from a unique viewpoint.

I would like to thank my mother and father for giving me the opportunity to tell this story of their success. I would also like to thank them for the greatest gift of all . . . life.

Acknowledgments

My deepest gratitude to all those from Cabela's who helped in so many ways to put this together, including but not limited to, Sharon Robison, David Draper, Kent Walton, Mark Nelsen, Cari Wamsley, Carmen Sebold, Amy Cabela, Jessica Cabela, Casey Smith, Rich Cabela, John Almanrode, Joe Arterburn, Mike Callahan and Tracie Garner. My thanks to Thomas Fensch and Paul and Peggy Eriksson. A special thanks to Teri Wolff and Dennis Highby and all those who were kind enough to share their thoughts and experiences. I would especially like to thank Shari, my wife, for her love and support during this process which sometimes seemed as if it would go on forever.

Introduction

by Brigadier General
Chuck Yeager
USAF, Retired

CABELA'S AS A COMPANY and the Cabela family as individuals have always had my highest regard. My admiration—and loyalty—started back in the company's early days when Cabela's was one of the few companies that would ship their products to overseas Armed Forces post offices. That may not sound like much, but if you've ever been stationed far from home, you know how important something like that can be.

Yes, I have a great deal of admiration for Dick, Mary and Jim—for their generosity toward the military and for everything they do for hunting, fishing and conservation. I'm just a typical hunter. I started hunting at age six when hunting was a source of meat for our table back in West

Virginia. As a lifelong hunter, I know how important it is for us—for all hunters—to support the great outdoor traditions of our country. Many may not realize how much the Cabela family does to support our treasured traditions. That is why I thought it was so appropriate that the Safari Club, at its 2001 convention, honored Dick with its prestigious C.J. McElroy Award and Mary (this makes me particularly proud, knowing what a fine woman she is) with the equally prestigious Diana Award.

To me, hunting brings out all that is good in our country. I really enjoy meeting people who like to hunt because they are, for the most part, truly honest and caring people. These are the kind of people who teach their kids to hunt and fish, the way I taught my children and my grandchildren. These are people whose values are sound and ethics are solid. The future of hunting depends on our young people and with what I've seen of the quality of young people getting involved today, I believe that future is bright.

It has been a pleasure to know the Cabelas and to watch their business grow from a small kitchen-table operation to a household name among outdoor enthusiasts throughout the world. Looking for a reason for their success, you can point to their reputation for high-quality products, reasonable prices and customer service that started out, and remains, a top priority. True, but it's really simpler than that. Cabela's has an attitude, a hard-to-describe something, that just makes sportsmen and women like to deal with them. I have come to know Cabela's well, having been at grand openings of many of the extraordinary retail stores, and have always come away impressed with the integrity and welcoming, friendly attitude of the employees. That, I think, is testimony to the founders of this wonderful company.

I hope you enjoy reading the Cabela's story. It is proof to all of us that the American dream can indeed come true.

Chronology

October 8, 1936 — Dick Cabela is born.

May 4, 1937 — Mary Kerns Cabela is born.

September 28, 1939 — Jim Cabela is born.

Early Winter 1961 — Dick buys fishing flies from Walker
  International.

Early Spring 1961 — First ad placed in *Casper Tribune*.

Late Summer 1961 — New ad placed in *Field and Stream*.

Late Fall — 3-page mimeographed "catalog" sent to existing customers.

Early Spring 1962 — Dick and Mary construct the first
  "warehouse" in their back yard.

Early 1963 — Jim moves back to Chappell to join Dick
  and Mary in Cabela's.

Early Spring 1963 — First catalog is mailed.

Early Spring 1964 — Company moves to basement of A.C. and Marian's furniture store.

Early 1965 — Cabela's is incorporated.

Early Spring 1965 — Company purchases former USDA building in Chappell.

Early Fall 1965 — Cabela's issues housewares catalog which fails miserably.

October, 1965 — Cabela's hires first full-time employee— Sharon Robison.

Late Summer 1966 — Cabela's mails out first Fall catalog.

Early Fall 1966 — Bert becomes Cabela's first security system.

Early Spring — Cabela's trades USDA building for former Legion Hall building.

Early 1968 — Dick and Jim begin drawing salaries from Cabela's.

September 1968 — Cabela's purchases old John Deere building and moves to Sidney.

1970 — Dick and Jim are jointly named Small Business Administration's "Man of the Year."

1971 — Cabela's begins accepting credit cards.

1973 — First Sidney warehouse is purchased next to the former John Deere building.

1975 — The first computer system makes the old recipe cards obsolete.

1979 — Company purchases old Sioux Army Depot building to be used as warehouses.

1983 — 1-800 number is initiated.

1984 — All shipping, receiving and storage is moved to warehouses ten miles northeast of Sidney.

December, 1985 — Company introduces travel agency for the outdoor enthusiast—Cabela's Outdoor Adventures.

1986 — Cabela's purchases old Rockwell International building in Kearney for telemarketing and retail space.

1991 — 75,000-square-foot flagship catalog showroom is built in Sidney.

1994 — Dick and Jim are inducted into Nebraska Business Hall of Fame.

1995 — The Cabela's CLUB Visa card is introduced

May, 1995 — Cabela's purchases taxidermy supply company, Van Dyke's.

January, 1998 — 120,000-square-foot corporate headquarters built in Sidney.

Spring 1998 — 700,000-square-foot distribution center is built in Prairie Du Chien, Wisconsin.

Spring 1998 — 150,000-square-foot showroom built in Owatonna, Minnesota.

October, 1998 — Cabela's.com is launched and is immediately profitable.

October, 1998 — 40,000-square-foot showroom is built next to the distribution center in Prairie Du Chien.

1999 — Cabela's is named Ernst and Young Entrepreneur of the Year in Retail/Consumer Products.

1999 — *Fortune Magazine* names Cabela's one of top 100 Best Companies to work for.

September, 1999 — 60,000-square-foot showroom is built in East Grand Forks, Minnesota.

2000 — Cabela's listed on the Forbes 500 Top Private Companies List.

Spring 2000 — 85,000-square-foot showroom is built in Mitchell, South Dakota.

July 2000 — First issue of *Cabela's Outfitter Journal* is released.

Fall 2000 — 200,000-square-foot showroom is built in Dundee, Michigan.

A
HISTORY

1. | *A Humble Dream*

CABELA'S WAS FOUNDED in 1961, but the story begins long before then when my father, Dick Cabela, was just a young boy. He was the first born of Marian and A.C. Cabela, who owned and operated a furniture store in the rural community of Chappell, Nebraska.

In the 1940's a young boy who found himself in a small town in the panhandle of Nebraska had to use his imagination for nearly all entertainment. The back yard of my father's childhood home seemed huge and could be turned into just about any setting—a desert; the mountains; or even an ocean with a bit of water and the frame of mind you can only find in one who has not yet begun to struggle for the attention of the opposite sex. Every day his exploration would take him farther from the comfort and safety of his home and after his younger brother Jim came into the world, he had a companion who could discover the wonders of a town and the untouched beauty and solitude of the Great Plains stretching forever beyond the last building.

My father's life as a youth was not *all* filled with freedom and fascination. Around that same time, polio had reached epidemic levels among children. Some of those infected died and others found themselves paralyzed. When my father was diagnosed, Marion and A.C. were informed that their son would never walk again.

My grandfather, A.C., struggled through the Great Depression and one of the results was that it was rare for him to display many emotions outwardly. He was the type of man who would rather chew on thumb tacks than let someone see him cry. One of the few times my grandmother remembered seeing her husband cry in over sixty years of marriage was the day they found out Dick had the crippling disease and had to leave their little boy in the hospital.

Dick eventually learned to walk with the aid of braces on his legs. Being the practical people they were, my grandparents believed the only way he was ever going to have a chance to walk without the braces was by having him walk as much as possible without any help. My grandmother said she spent many mornings crying as she watched her baby, on his way to school, fall down three or four times before he even made it to the end of the driveway. She needed all of her strength to keep herself from running outside and carrying her child, burdened with leg braces, all the way to the schoolyard.

Even as a kid, my father was determined to succeed. His perseverance eventually paid off—his legs strengthened and he joyfully discarded the braces he had known for so long.

As I recount these rigors my father had to overcome as a child, I begin to understand why he has been so successful in the other facets of his life. I do not know that I will ever fully understand the strength and courage my dad was forced to embrace at such an early age. Of all the things our parents pass on to us I hope some of the courage that little boy with polio had will be passed on to me.

The few stories of his childhood my father has shared with me have nothing to do with polio. Hunting rabbits, fishing for whatever he could catch and camping in the back yard with his brother, Jim, are far more prevalent in his boyhood memories.

He also remembers testing his business savvy long before he ever knew which path he would follow: One of the neighbor kids had a dog which had recently given birth to a litter of puppies. Young Dick wanted one of those puppies pretty badly, but he had no money. Of his meager possessions all he believed he could afford to trade were three rusty fishhooks he carried in his overused, under-supplied fishing pack. Those fish hooks had caught plenty of fish and their well-used, rust-colored look was *more* than enough proof. Dick really wanted the puppy so he reluctantly handed over his proven commodities. Both boys bragged to their friends for weeks about the great trade they had made with the other, each believing he had gotten the better bargain.

Dick may have believed he had made the deal of the century, but he failed to consider the entire price. What had not occurred to him was the slight possibility that his parents might not want him to have the dog as much as he wanted to have it. A.C. was a little upset, to say the least, and as far as he was concerned, his son had gotten the worse end of the deal. After all, *he* did not want a mangy beast running around the house and *he* didn't want to have to be the one to take care of it. He finally conceded that having the puppy might teach Dick some responsibility and allowed his son to keep his new pet.

As the years progressed, Dick did learn responsibility. He attended a private Catholic high school in Sidney, Nebraska—St. Patrick's. He then went on to Regis College in Denver, returning to Chappell after a few years. In 1955, he married Mary Kerns and they had their first child the following year.

By the time he was twenty-five, Dick and Mary were the proud parents of four children. Dick made his living as manager of the small furniture store owned by his parents. A portion of the success Cabela's has achieved can be traced back to Marian and A.C. The values of hard work and determination Dick and his younger brother, Jim, needed to be successful were often displayed by their parents as they brought up six children and ran a business of their own.

Cabela's began with a single idea, a conception my father took a chance on. He didn't know if it would pay off, but knew he had to try. So, like others before him, Dick Cabela decided to become an entrepreneur and took an idea from his mind and acted on it, setting into motion the first step that would turn a humble man's dream into "The World's Foremost Outfitter."

In January of 1961, Dick accompanied his father to Kansas City and then to Chicago to purchase some furniture to sell at A.C.'s small furniture store. They left Chappell in the evening during a snowstorm and drove the whole night, without sleeping, all the way to Kansas City. They spent a few hours there and purchased some upholstered furniture, grabbed a bite to eat and drove on to Chicago. There were no interstate systems at the time, so they had to travel the entire distance on highways, many of them snow covered and slick. They were on the road, without rest, for approximately twenty hours.

Once they arrived in Chicago, they headed straight to the Chicago Furniture Mart and then on to the Merchandise Mart to buy furniture and other goods for the furniture store. When they had finished their furniture purchases, father and son moved on to the Navy Pier, where they searched for gift items to sell in Chappell.

At the Navy Pier Housewares Show, in a far-back corner, my dad spotted a booth housing a small company called Walker International. They decided to take a closer look and discovered most of the merchandise being sold was Japanese fishing equipment.

Dad noticed most of the products Walker International sold were extremely inexpensive. As he browsed through the tackle in the booth, a particular product caught his eye. He spied some hand-tied flies being sold at a ridiculously low price. A mere $2.25 for a whole gross of assorted flies was just too good a deal to pass up. (In today's market a single fly can cost two dollars or more.) He just knew he would make a nice profit if he could sell the flies at the current market price.

After convincing his father they could sell the tiny flies, he decided to take the risk and bought twenty gross. He would try to sell them in the hardware department of his father's furniture store. At that time, Dick had no idea the forty-five dollars spent on those flies would be the initial investment for a company which would eventually be known around the globe as the World's Foremost Outfitter. But as we all know, overnight success is rarely achieved in any industry.

A few months passed and not a single fly was sold through the store. My dad told me he began to wonder if the money he'd spent on those flies had been a wise investment.

Habitually, he visited Wieland's Drugstore where he spent his time perusing issues of *Field and Stream* and drinking coffee. The outdoor magazine which had so often given him entertainment and information was about to give him an idea that, through many years of hard work, would bring his humble vision to extraordinary realities.

On a day like any other day, Dick Cabela ambled up the street to Wieland's Drugstore, located in downtown Chappell, to have a cup of coffee. As he sat and leisurely sipped the hot coffee, he picked up a copy of *Field and Stream* and proceeded to do a little reading.

This was not the first copy of *Field and Stream* he had ever opened to read, nor would it be his last. However, on that fateful day, he was completely unaware that doing so would give him an idea which would eventually change his life.

Normally, Dick opened a magazine from the front cover and began reading there. He doesn't remember why he did it but, on that particular day he took the magazine and opened it from the back cover. His eyes immediately fixed upon pages full of classified ads and he wondered why he had not noticed any of them before. He read the ads and saw others offering a number of items including such things as dogs, knives, and even worms, for sale.

As he continued to read through the space ads, Dick envisioned that a profit could be made by selling fishing products through classified ads. After all, if anglers were willing to buy live bait through the mail, they should be willing to buy items that would not perish before arriving in their mail boxes. For example, anglers might be interested in purchasing low-cost, hand-tied flies Dick just happened to have an abundance of in his possession.

Shortly after he'd read the issue of *Field and Stream*, my father and my mother, Mary, took a trip to Wyoming. Mom visited her mother in Casper and Dad went fishing at a place called the Hole in the Wall Gang Canyon, located in the Wyoming Powder River Basin, which Butch Cassidy, The Sundance Kid and their gang used as a hideout. While fishing, he was surrounded by many other anglers, but thought little of it.

During the same fishing trip they traveled to the Miracle Mile of the North Platte River, below Pathfinder Dam, where he was surrounded by many other fishermen, most of them fly-fishing. He quickly determined that his father's furniture store in Chappell, Nebraska was not the ideal location from which to sell the hand-tied flies. A place like Wyoming, where there appeared to be more people who fly-fished, offered a better market for the flies.

During the ride back to Chappell, Dad shared his idea with someone else for the first time. Out of the blue, he told Mom he was seriously thinking about starting a fishing business using space ads. It would have to be a part-time hobby, as the family income came from his full-time job as manager of his father's furniture store. Mom never questioned, because she knew he was an eternal optimist and would surely succeed.

Dad bought every last one of the flies from the furniture store. He now had a tiny business of his own. The inexpensive flies became Cabela's first stocked merchandise. They were kept in the pantry near the kitchen table. Mom had to shove them in between the sugar sack and the cornflakes box.

Although my grandfather, A.C. Cabela, was skeptical at first, he did not express doubts to my father. He merely wished him luck and hoped he would succeed.

Once while I was talking to my grandfather he revealed his first gut feeling about Dad's plan to start his own business—a fishing company:

"I thought he was crazy to think he could make money selling fishing flies using classified ads. I didn't say that to him though. I was sure it wouldn't work, but believed he could learn one of life's lessons by trying. I finally told him what I had thought, several years later—after he had proved me wrong."

Unaware of his father's skepticism and without an ounce of his own, Dick proceeded with his plan. Failure was not an option. He was going to move onto the next step regardless of what others believed. The opinions of his loved ones were very important to him, but he was determined to carry through with his new venture.

The first decision to be made was where to place a classified ad that would be read by a high number of consumers interested in hand-tied flies. He instantly thought of Wyoming, where he had seen so many fly fishermen. As a result, he placed his very first ad in a Wyoming newspaper, the *Casper Tribune*:

12 hand-tied fishing flies for $1, postage paid.

Unfortunately, only one order came from that ad, from Mrs. Ernest Lindahl of Casper—the first Cabela's customer.

Dad had not sold any flies in the Chappell furniture store and only one set through his ad in the *Casper Tribune*. Many people, including myself, might have given up after such a lack of interest. There had been virtually no response. Dad told me he wondered if he was going to be stuck with 2,879 fishing flies for his own personal tackle box. He liked to fish, but his tackle box just wasn't big enough.

He could have quit and accepted the fact that consumers from Casper, Wyoming, plenty of them avid fly fishermen, either did not read the classified ads or were unwilling to purchase fishing flies through the mail. Maybe the possibility of selling fishing equipment that way was not such a great idea. Anyone who knows Dick Cabela knows he is not a quitter, and he believed his idea was sound.

Admittedly, Dick was disappointed by the lack of orders from his first ad, but he did not give up. Yet, he realized ads in the *Casper Tribune* were not going to reach enough interested consumers. He needed another outlet to sell his fishing flies.

Dad quickly moved on to Plan B and ran an ad in *Field and Stream*, the very magazine he was reading when he initially had the idea of selling fishing flies through classified ads. Still convinced that if others could sell live bait, such as worms, grubs and hellgrammites through *Field and Stream*, he could certainly sell quality hand-tied flies, using space ads.

He decided not to run the same ad he had placed in the *Casper Tribune*. That one had resulted in just a single order. He would have to be a little more creative to find better success with a new ad.

The revised ad was not all that different from the first one. It took up the same amount of space and was just as simple, but with a few changes. The second ad read:

> 5 hand-tied fishing flies . . . FREE. 25 cents
> postage and handling.

This one ran in a late-summer 1961 edition of *Field and Stream*. The word "free," he knew has always been a strong word for American consumers.

In the fall, Dad and Grandpa returned to the Chicago Merchandise Mart for the fall furniture show and the house-wares show at the Navy Pier. While he was in Chicago Dad phoned Mom, who had stayed home in Chappell with their four children. Her voice was filled with excitement when she told him that twenty-three orders for the flies had arrived that day. The ad in *Field and Stream* had begun to show some potential. Dick knew this was only the beginning:

"I was extremely excited. We actually had customers. I knew I couldn't just sit around and hope for the best. I had to explore other avenues. I placed the same ad in two more magazines, *Outdoor Life* and *Sports Afield*, spending all our profits and then some."

The doors to success were slowly opening. With Dick and Mary's hard work and support of each other, the future World's Foremost Outfitter was beginning to show promise.

These early orders arrived in a little less than first-class fashion. Most of them came in envelopes with copies of the ad, and usually with quarters or dimes and nickels taped to a small piece of cardboard. On several occasions, Dad and Mom remember receiving twenty-five pennies taped to a piece of cardboard, with a request for the free flies.

As the orders arrived, Mom typed the names and addresses of each new customer on recipe cards and placed them alphabetically in a shoebox, really not knowing why

they did so. The names turned out to be their first customer
database. At that time, they were naive about the way a mail-
order business should be run. Their reason for keeping the
cards was "just in case."

Dick and Mary filled the orders using their own home-
made plastic bags for packaging each order of five assorted
fishing flies. They didn't know where they could get small
plastic bags and even if they had known, they could not afford
to buy them with the tiny profit the small business, named
Cabela's Distributing at that time, was bringing in.

The small bags were made from the plastic cover bags
used by dry cleaners. Mom and Dad saved these every time a
load of clothes was returned to them. They took the plastic
bags and cut them into small squares. After cutting the
correct number of squares to correspond with the orders they
had to fill, they would place an assortment of five flies in the
center of the plastic square. Once the flies were in place, they
would fold the squares around them and staple the folds shut,
forming a small bag. These were put in an envelope and taken
to the Chappell post office to be shipped to the customers.

This may seem like an awful lot of work for a mere
twenty-five cents a piece, but the satisfaction of knowing
success could be reached was well worth the labor. My father
always pushed his children to work hard for what we wanted
and seldom gave any handouts. He has often told us we would
appreciate our accomplishments much more if we worked for
them ourselves. When we were younger we thought he was
just trying to trick us into doing our chores or punishing us.

As the years roll on, the crazy things our parents said seem to make more sense with each passing day.

As the ad read, each customer paid twenty-five cents for postage and handling; the five hand-tied flies were free. Each fly cost the company one and a half cents, each envelope a half cent and a first-class postage stamp six cents. In the beginning, labor was free—Dick and Mary did all of the work themselves.

A single order cost them a grand total of fourteen cents. The profit of eleven cents on every order soon paid for the ads. Cabela's was now out of the red and into the black. Their dream of having a profitable business was beginning to look as if it were within reach.

Dad realized he now had a customer base—that is, if a few dozen qualify as a customer base. These few customers who had bought hand-tied fishing flies through the mail might very well be interested in purchasing other fishing equipment.

As a consequence he returned to Walker International's small booth still buried back in that corner of the Navy Pier housewares show, where he bought a plethora of other fishing products hoping his new customers would find them appealing. He purchased items such as hooks, lures, reels, and bamboo fly rods. He risked all of the company's profits as well as some funds from his own pocket on these new products.

Always a strong believer in the power of simple word-of-mouth, my father was confident that if he offered quality products along with quality service, a few customers would tell their outdoor friends, who would tell their friends, and so on and so forth. Although he knew word-of-mouth advertising was effective, he could never have predicted just how powerful the words of outdoor enthusiasts would actually be. Cabela's has always sold recreational equipment and only sells a limited number of items which could be considered essential. Considering that almost all advertising for the company has taken place in the last decade, it is easy to see how the voices of the first few Cabela's customers echoed through the hunting, fishing and outdoor community with tremendous velocity and longevity.

$\mathcal{2}_\circ$ | *First Catalogs*

WHEN DICK RETURNED from Chicago to Chappell with the new merchandise in the fall of 1961, he and Mary decided to make up a three-page mimeographed "catalog" to send to their customers. With each shipment of a new order for flies, they included one of these small catalogs. This is a typical direct-mail practice still popular today.

Mary doesn't remember following any instructions:

"We had never even heard of typical direct-mail practices. We just thought this was the best way to let our customers know we had other items to offer. We hoped some of them would want to buy a few of the new products. If they had not, we would have been stuck with more fishing equipment than we could ever use. I remember feeling a little nervous and hoping that if things didn't go well, all our children would enjoy fishing. That way, the equipment would at least be used."

The highest-priced item in their three mimeographed sheets was a Model #R619 Deluxe pellet rifle with adjustable sights and a shoulder strap. It cost the customer a mere $9.95. The lowest-priced items in the catalog were nylon-coated wire leaders with stainless steel snaps, which were priced at a nickel each.

Today it would be impossible to find those items at such prices but in 1961 the Cabela's Catalog prices were lower than you could find almost anywhere. In order for their small business to compete in the market, Dad realized they would have to sustain a very small profit margin.

Though inflation has caused the prices to change since 1961, Dick continuously assures their customers: "We still sell high quality merchandise at a fair price and back it with our 100% satisfaction guarantee."

This kind of guarantee, which Cabela's promises, was unheard of in 1961 and has become world famous. From day one, Dick has believed that in order to be successful you must satisfy the customer, despite the small losses you may suffer.

Many companies offer a guarantee, but the promise Cabela's made was quite rare. As long as a single customer does not abuse the guarantee, and sometimes even if one does, Cabela's will refund the money or replace the item to their customers with no questions asked, despite the date of purchase or condition of the product.

One might think this guarantee to the consumer would invite abuse, but Dick and Mary knew, despite what the front pages of the newspapers said, the majority of the people on God's earth are good, honest people.

At the bottom of the third page of that first mimeographed catalog the customer could read this guarantee and know there was virtually no risk to them if they purchased a product from Cabela's. The guarantee read as follows:

> Satisfaction guaranteed. All items listed carry our money back guarantee. If you are not completely satisfied, simply return the merchandise and your money will be promptly refunded.

Cabela's guarantee still stands today just as it did in 1961. Dad contends that this outstanding customer service has been the backbone of Cabela's—a bone that bends but doesn't break. There is one story which he has been known to recount when expressing the customer service that Cabela's embodies:

"We have a loyal customer who has purchased from the company for more than twenty years and over that time has spent over $12,000. This customer had purchased a pair of hunting boots from Cabela's. Four years later, he returned the boots with virtually zero tread left on the soles, complaining that they just didn't fit right. Though it was obvious the boots had been worn many times during the four years the customer had owned them, he was given his choice of a replacement pair or a refund. This customer was given the benefit of the doubt that his boots just did not feel right for four years. He is still a loyal customer and has never abused the policy other than this one incident with the boots."

By this time, Cabela's inventory had grown to the point where Mom could no longer keep the items in her pantry. To provide for this much-needed space, they purchased the company's very first warehouse in 1962, a small ten-foot-by-ten-foot tin shed that Mom and Dad had to put together. Since all the orders were filled from their kitchen table they had to locate this tiny warehouse nearby in the backyard.

For the first year and a half, Dick and Mary were able to handle the business alone from their kitchen table. However, in 1962 they did hire a temporary typist who helped with the labeling and catalog preparation. This young high school girl, Susie Gerber, would cross the street to Mom and Dad's home after school and work for a few hours. In addition, she also baby-sat the couple's first four children, Nancy, Geri, Teri, and Rich.

Working full-time at my grandfather's furniture store, Dad could work on his own business only during the evening hours. Thus, it was not uncommon for him and Mom to spend the entire night filling orders. Two or three in the morning was the normal end to a day's work, leaving very little time for rest.

As the end of 1962 approached, it became apparent to both Dad and Mom that the demands of their new business venture required full-time attention, even though only twenty-three checks had been written in the entire month of

December. There was not enough profit for Dad to quit his job at Grandfather's furniture store, and the demands of their four small children prohibited Mom from giving the business full-time attention. They needed to find some help.

Early in 1963 my dad asked my uncle Jim to join him and Mom in their new company. At the time, Jim lived in Denver and was starting a new career in banking. With some trepidation, he left a fairly comfortable Denver lifestyle and moved back to his hometown of Chappell to join Cabela's.

The business was not bringing in enough profit for any of them to draw a salary. Dick, Mary and Jim re-invested every penny of profit back into their growing business. Dick continued to make his living working at his father's furniture store to provide for his growing family. Jim would run the company during the day and in turn received half of the business from Dick and Mary. To save expenses, Jim moved in with his parents, A.C. and Marian, and lived on his meager National Guard pay.

As well as being the year Jim joined the company, 1963 also marked the first year in which Cabela's Distributing retired the mimeographed sheets and mailed out their first full-fledged catalog.

The catalog was entirely black-and-white from cover to cover. The very top of the front cover read, CABELA'S WHOLESALE CATALOG. The middle of the front cover sported a black-and-white drawing of a fly fisherman reeling in a wild trout jumping from the running waters of a tranquil river. Below the fly fisherman, customers were informed as to what could be found in the catalog. In bold letters it read: **Fishing Equipment and Supplies.**

Upon opening the front cover, the customer was asked, "Why Buy from Cabela Distributing?" Cabela's went on to explain why, as follows:

> If you want to SAVE money and get better service, then BUY from CABELA DISTRIB-UTING. Check these features:
> SMALL TOWN LOCATION—enabling us to operate under extremely low overhead, thus making our prices highly competitive.
> MASSIVE BUYING for lower prices.
> NO MIDDLEMAN—direct factory buying.
> PLUS very small profit margin.
> CHECK OUR OVERALL PRICES—item for item we are the lowest priced in the nation.
> WE ARE HERE TO SERVE YOU!
> We are positive you will be pleased with our Fine Quality Merchandise.
> ORDERING BY MAIL—Saves you money, it's convenient, and fun! We process all orders immediately, you get fast service, plus the finest quality merchandise at the lowest possible price.

This first catalog was fifty-five pages long and contained almost nothing but fishing equipment and supplies as the front cover promised. However, there was one item on page fifty-one that stood out from the rest. The only product a Cabela's customer could purchase from the catalog that was not related to fishing was a set of fifty maple golf tees for twenty-five cents.

I suppose it may be possible for golf tees to be fishing-related for an angler with a creative mind. If an angler really wanted to they could use a golf tee as a small bobber while fishing for extremely small game fish.

By 1964 Cabela's inventory had grown to the point where the small backyard warehouse was not enough to store all of their products. As a result, they decided to move the entire small operation to the basement of their father's furniture store. The building had been switched over to natural gas and they removed an obsolete fuel tank in order to give them more room. The extra space served the company's needs for the time being.

If their inventory was to continue to grow, Cabela's needed to find new product suppliers. The few items Walker International offered could no longer meet the needs of the slow but steady growth of the business. They needed to go to established name-brand manufacturers and hope these manufacturers would sell to their tiny new company. The opportunity to meet with a number of these companies presented itself in August of 1964 at the AFTMA (American Fishing Tackle Manufacturers Association) Convention in Chicago.

Mary Cabela remembers that first trip to the AFTMA Convention quite well:

"We drove all day and all night from Chappell to Chicago for the AFTMA Convention. I was pregnant with Chuck, who was born three months later, in November. We went to several name-brand companies and no one would talk to us because we were not truly established, as far as they were concerned. We finally, very discouraged, went to Garcia Corporation in the old Bismark Hotel where we talked to Gene England, who believed we had a chance to be a successful business. He took a gamble and sold us Garcia products on a cash-only basis and a minimum qualifying distributor price. This opened the door. The next year four other companies came on board. No salesmen would call on us because we were too far removed from everyone's territory, so all purchasing had to be done at the yearly AFTMA Convention each August. We finally became well enough known after a few years and were able to buy on credit with terms from most fishing tackle manufacturers."

At this point, Cabela's was not in the retail business, but locals would periodically enter the basement of the furniture store and attempt to purchase an item or two. Cabela's did not advertise to these local retail consumers, nor did they discourage them, and word of mouth brought in more and more retail customers. Even before the company relocated to the basement of the furniture store, consumers would, ever so often, come to the Cabela home in search of the perfect lure or bamboo fishing rod. Before Cabela's was founded, there were very few sources of quality fishing equipment in the rural community of Chappell or the surrounding areas.

Due to the fact that Dad, Mom, and Jim reinvested every bit of profit back into it, the business grew steadily for those first few trying years. In 1965 they were incorporated and Cabela Distributing became Cabela's, Incorporated.

They determined the basement of the furniture store was no longer large enough to satisfy their company's needs so as a result they purchased the former USDA building, which was located directly across the street from A.C. Cabela's furniture store. They hoped this new property would meet the demands of their growing business.

The 1965 catalog embodied the success Cabela's had experienced in the previous years. The catalog had grown from fifty-five pages in 1963 to seventy-six pages in 1965. The customers could purchase new items such as camping gear, archery equipment and products for their firearms, as well as everything that was available in the 1963 and 1964 catalogs, including those maple golf tees. The first seventeen pages offered nothing but fishing reels. It was safe to say that Cabela's inventory had grown immensely since those few hand-tied fishing flies Dick purchased in 1961.

Just inside the front cover of the 1965 catalog was a letter to the customers thanking them for their loyal business:

Dear Sportsmen:

As one of the leading mail-order concerns it gives us great pleasure to bring you our 1965 catalogue.

We wish to take this opportunity to thank

all of our loyal customers for their past patron-age in helping make 1964 our greatest year, a 500% increase in volume over 1963.

It gives us deep satisfaction knowing we have made so many good friends throughout this wonderful country.

As you leaf through our catalog you will find that again in 1965 we lead the industry in bringing lowest prices, better service and, most of all, customer satisfaction.

We have sacrificed our profits to bring you the greatest selection of goods we have ever had, at the lowest prices we have ever had. We urge you to compare our prices. We will not be undersold. Our quality is the finest plus every item carries a double guarantee, both ours and the manufacturer's.

Thanking you,
Cabela's, Inc.

Fall and winter were extremely slow periods for Cabela's in the early and mid 1960's. The reason was quite simple, really—more people fished in the spring and summer than in the colder seasons. To try to build their volume of business in the fall, they decided to send a housewares flyer to their customers. Some of the items included in it were cedar-scented clothing bags, diaper-pin lubricators, and check protectors. However, the customers were anglers and outdoorsmen and had very little interest in these gimmicky products.

Dick refers to this flyer as his "first big mistake":

"I deviated from the first rule of marketing: 'Stick with what you know.' We tried a housewares flyer. We mailed thousands of these flyers which included genuine-fake leather coasters, egg slicers, clown faced doorknob covers, and serving spoons with a thermostat in the handle. I forgot my name was Cabela and made a brief attempt at being Harriet Carter. Almost forty years later, I think we still have some exploding golf balls in a corner of the basement. I had been an Eagle Scout. I loved hunting. I would rather go fishing than eat, and if my mother would have permitted it, I would have lived in a tent in the back yard. Whatever possessed me to think I could sell housewares?"

It didn't take long for them to realize their customers had no use for the items they had tried to sell in that doomed flyer. Never again would they forget their last name was Cabela and their core products were for fishing, hunting and outdoor activities.

As their business grew, it demanded more and more of their time. Since they weren't drawing a salary, but putting everything back into the company, Dick continued to work at his father's furniture store while Jim ran the day-to-day affairs.

The company's growth rate made it impossible to run without help. In October of 1965 Cabela's hired its first full-time employee. That employee's name was Sharon Robison. Still employed with the company, driving forty-five miles each

way every day, from Julesburg, Colorado, she proves to be a
very loyal employee. Sharon recalls her first impressions of the
company and her beginning years as an associate at Cabela's:

"I was a newly married teenager living in Chappell,
Nebraska, when a friend suggested I put in my application at
Cabela's. His brothers owned this new company and they
needed temporary assistance to perform physical inventory. I
put on a business dress, heels and pearls, and prepared
mentally to put myself through the rigors of my first job inter-
view since graduating from business college. I had called for
an appointment and was told to come in the front door.
When I arrived I was a bit surprised that the 20 x 60 space was
filled with shelves except for a small area in the back which
had several tables surrounded by piles of cardboard boxes. In
the corner was an antique multi-cubby-holed, rolltop desk.

"Mr. James Cabela was hard at work, so I introduced
myself and gritted my teeth for his first question. He asked me
to write my name and phone number on a slip of paper, which
I did. I handed him the information and it immediately disap-
peared into one of the cubby holes in the massive desk. Mr.
Cabela told me 'thanks, we'll call you.' I was certain that I'd
never hear from him again.

"I did get a call back from Jim Cabela. I started work the
week after I applied (I guess that rolltop desk was more organized than outward appearances would indicate). My assigned
task the first day of work was to affix labels to a mail piece."

Sharon Robison began her career at Cabela's around the
same time the brothers decided to mail their gimmicky

housewares flyer. She recalls her reaction to her first responsibilities:

"Mailing that flyer in 1965 required mega man hours, as it was completely a hand process. The names were manually typed on a sheet of paper which was perforated to accommodate 33 labels. These sheets would be torn into the individual labels and sorted by state. To speed this sorting process someone had taken a piece of thin board and printed out a space for each of the states in alphabetical sequence. Then the labels were affixed to the mail piece, bundled and taken to the post office. Sticking on labels was the task I was assigned my first day at Cabela's. The backside of the labels was a re-moist 'spit and stick.' I was provided with a sponge and became a human label affixer. At the end of that first eight-hour day I was quite resigned that I would be seeking other employment soon. I couldn't imagine that a company crazy enough to pay me for slapping labels on a mail piece all day was going to be around for very long. But after a few days it was like a new relationship . . . I felt a desire to stick around just to see what was going to happen next!"

The 1966 catalog was a bit more impressive than the previous year's. It had grown another seven pages, to eighty-three. The cover sported a jubilant fly fisherman in a red-checkered shirt netting a plump rainbow trout. Although there was still not full color, the cover of the 1966 catalog was a step up from the pure black-and-white cover of the 1963 catalog.

A few of the most notable new items included in the

1966 catalog were a golf umbrella, golf balls (supposedly to go along with those maple golf tees that so many anglers keep in their tackle boxes). On the last page of the catalog one item sticks out even more than the maple golf tees, an item that every angler absolutely, positively must have. The final page of the 1966 catalog offered seven- eight- and nine-foot pool tables.

Today it is easy for me to make light of certain items in the catalogs because the only Cabela's, Incorporated most customers have ever known has been more or less strictly devoted to serving the needs and desires of anglers, hunters and outdoor enthusiasts who share the same passion for the wild as I do.

In reality, Cabela's was only a few years old and any mistake could have had major consequences. My dad makes fun of the housewares flyer now, but he found nothing amusing about "losing his shirt," as he puts it, at the time when the items in the flyer were a complete failure.

Dick and Jim were struggling to learn what their customers wanted. As it turned out, most Cabela's customers are and always have been quite similar to the two brothers in their love for outdoor adventures. The golf and billiard products were not as far from outdoor products as the housewares items, but they were still not the hunting, fishing, camping and other outdoor products Cabela's is known for.

As the 1965 catalog did, the one for 1966 also invited Cabela's customers to browse through it in a brief letter on the first page:

Dear Sportsman:

It gives us great pleasure to present to you our 1966 catalog.

As you leaf through this catalog you will find that again in 1966 we lead the industry in bringing you the lowest prices, plus better service and most of all customer satisfaction.

We are especially proud of our fishing "outfits". We think we have made a first in the fishing tackle industry. We have, for the first time, assembled a group of "fishing outfits" without a bunch of cheap junk that isn't usable. For the first time you can buy an outfit with the confidence that every item will be of highest quality.

Every item we sell is guaranteed to satisfy 100% or your money back (no exceptions).

If you have bought from us before, we thank you for the business entrusted us in the past, and we look forward to serving you for many years to come. If you have not bought from us, please give us a try. We shall do our best to deserve your confidence.

Cabela's, Inc.

The 1966 catalog sported twelve of the fishing outfits mentioned in the letter. Recently, as I browsed through the pages showing these outfits, the quality and quantity of equipment offered and the low prices at which they were offered, caught me off guard. I had to remind myself that I was reading a catalog printed in 1966. I almost picked up the phone and tried to order one of these fishing outfits.

As a fly fisherman who is unskilled in the art of fly-tying, I purchase all of my equipment. I was naturally impressed by the fly-fishing outfit that could be purchased for only $9.99.

As well as a black-and-white photo of the outfit, the catalog gave a brief description:

> Complete balanced outfit. Bronson Regal 360 Single Action Reel with on-off click-type drag. Lightweight black anodized aluminum frame. H-1 Regal quality 2-piece fly rod, made of finest quality tubular nylon reinforced glass. Screw locking reel seat-cork grip. Complete fly casting kit contains 16 proven flies and poppers, balanced Gladding Fly Line, Weber Tapered Leader, bag of split shot, and free fly casting instruction.

Inflation has made finding a single item on that list for $9.99 virtually impossible today. Even if we take inflation into account the price was more than reasonable in 1966.

The success of the 1966 spring catalog once again surpassed all previous catalogs. At this point, Dick and Jim were not really thinking in terms of growth rate and were just happy to keep their business alive. The growth rate was, in fact, well in the high hundreds as more and more outdoor enthusiasts discovered Cabela's. Much of the success of the 1966 spring catalog was due to the quantity and quality of the fishing products offered in the book. The Cabela's catalog was also starting to make a name for itself with outdoor-lovers across the country as a place where they could buy quality merchandise at a fair price.

As the temperature began to drop and the leaves slightly changed color, Dick and Jim remembered the doomed flyer they had sent out to their customers the year before. There was not a chance they would send out another housewares flyer to those customers who had rejected the first one. Yet, they had to address the problem of the drastic slump in sales during the fall.

Naturally, they decided to stick with what they knew. Neither Dick nor Jim knew much about the housewares products they had attempted to sell the year before. However they both had a strong passion for the outdoors and knew enjoying the outdoors and being a participant in nature was an important part of their lives and should be experienced in fall and winter as much as, if not more than in spring and summer. They were so sure their customers shared this passion for the outdoor world they decided to mail a fall catalog featuring products aimed at fall and winter outdoor adventures. Thus, in 1966, the first Cabela's fall catalog was born.

The cover of the 1966 fall catalog presented a scene of a peaceful mountain lake reflecting the fall colors of different shades of yellow and green from a serene valley connecting the lake to three giant peaks reaching high into a clear blue sky. The cover represented the beauty of the outdoors that the two brothers and their customers always enjoyed being a part of.

Many of the drawings and pictures on Cabela's catalog covers over the years have epitomized the lives of the Cabelas and their loyal patrons. The Cabelas, like most of their customers, are great lovers of the wild. What's more, they are not merely spectators of nature but are an important part of nature's beautiful and unavoidable circle of life. Personally, I have always looked forward to receiving each new catalog not only for the gear but to admire the next cover image which captures the beauty of the natural world outdoor enthusiasts hold so dear.

The risk they took with this 1966 fall catalog could have meant certain doom for the brothers and their company. If their customers had refused it as whole-heartedly as they had rejected the housewares flyer the year before, they may never have rebounded from the loss. However, Dick and Jim bet the farm that their customers were as passionate as they were about fall outdoor activities. With the immediate success of the 1966 catalog they were proven to be correct.

Though they had risked nearly everything to produce this catalog, the decision was not made blindly. The 1965 catalog contained two pages of items normally associated with fall outdoor activities and these items had sold successfully. The fact that customers had made purchases from that very limited selection reassured the brothers there would be inter-est in an entire fall catalog.

They decided to counteract possible risk by filling fifteen of the thirty-three pages with fishing equipment. They knew their patrons were interested in fishing, and thought that any lack of interest in the new products could be offset by the appeal of the reliable fishing equipment. Interestingly, today the business the company does in the fall exceeds the business generated in the spring.

The first seven pages of the 1966 fall catalog contained nothing but archery equipment. The traditional archer would especially enjoy flipping through them. The first conventional compound bow would not be introduced for another four or five years. Archery has gone through many changes since the 1960's. Technology has created bows with higher power requiring less physical exertion and arrows which fly farther and straighter. With the increased popularity of bow hunting and competition, manufacturers of archery equipment scramble to design and present better quality items than their competitors. Today, Cabela's mails out catalogs wholly devoted to archery equipment.

The archer as well as firearm enthusiasts would find the next ten pages of the 1966 fall catalog very appealing. Though the selection of goods offered in these ten pages was humble compared to the vast selection Cabela's now offers, the outdoor participant would have easily found numerous items they simply *couldn't live* without. The consumers were offered a decent collection of hunting knives, optics, and sleeping bags, as well as a moderate assortment of clothing and other camping and hunting accessories, including compasses, gun blue creme and an umbrella tent.

About this same time, Cabela's acquired their very first security system. This first "alarm system" was known to have chased vendors and freight men from the premises and, according to Sharon Robison, had to be taken for regular walks. The first, and the most feared security system at Cabela's was Burt, a 90-pound German Shepherd.

Jim Cabela's dog had turned out to be such an exceptional guard dog that he was given the run of the building during the nighttime hours when the business was closed. During business hours he had to be kept in the back to ensure that he did not chase away vendors or potential customers. Penny for penny and pound for pound, Burt was considered the best security system Cabela's ever owned. It was a sad day when Burt finally retired.

Jack Fuson was one of the first sales representatives ever to call on Cabela's and has formed a great relationship with the owners. He definitely remembers Burt:

"I started calling on Cabela's in Chappell in the early 1960's. The impression of the first time I ever called on them will always stick with me. I knocked on the door and at the same time their dog hit the door barking. I think that was the day my hair turned gray."

In 1966 the brothers hired two more full-time employees for a grand total of three. Alene Stutzman joined the company in January and Pearl Kayton joined in June. Their major responsibilities in the beginning included taking and filling orders, typing up mailing orders, acting as retail clerks whenever a local consumer would stroll in hoping to purchase an item . . . and of course, taking Burt for walks.

At this point in the company's history everything was done by hand. Information on every customer was kept on 3 x 5-inch recipe cards, which were sorted in alphabetical order and stored in boxes. The consumer's name and address were then typed on four-part gum labels. There were forty perforated labels on four 8 x 10 sheets with three sheets of carbon paper separating the sheets. These layered label sheets made it possible for them to produce four mailing labels by typing each customer's name only once.

Mary Cabela gives us a brief impression of their first customer base, whose names were recorded on recipe cards:

"We did this from the beginning, not nearly knowing why we were doing it, but it gave us our first customer-based file. They were filed in shoe boxes in our pantry. I typed all names on the recipe cards from day one with Mrs. Ernest Lindahl being the first customer."

Their customer base was growing very rapidly. Even though typing a customer's name and address just once provided enough mailing labels to last an entire year or more, typing mailing labels consumed a great amount of time. After the children were put to bed, Mary recalls spending many late nights doing nothing but typing mailing labels for the catalogs.

Mom remembers one late night in particular when she was working diligently at the typewriter producing mailing labels from the 3 x 5 recipe cards. There was a window, just above the folding table where she was working. Her only companion in the building that night was Burt, who was lying indifferently on the cool floor behind her chair. To this day, Mom does not know what caused Burt's sudden change in attitude. Maybe there was a person or other creature outside that window; this she will never know. The German Shepherd, which only a few moments before provided her with the comfort of security, gave her a scare she would never forget:

"Burt must have seen, smelled or heard something outside that window, because he flew over my shoulder onto the folding table with such furor that I initially thought he had gone mad and was attacking me before I realized his ferocity was aimed at something outside the window and not at me."

Once the mailing labels were all typed and the season had come to mail out the next shipment of catalogs, hours were spent preparing the catalogs for shipment. The gum labels in the late 1960's were not self-adhesive, as they are now. Dick, Jim, Mary and their employees would have to tear each label around its perforated edge and lick or wet the back of it before affixing it onto a catalog. Catalogs would then be sorted according to state.

Once, shortly before it was time to mail out another shipment of catalogs, Jim had instructed a new employee to tear up the labels and sort them. What he meant was to tear them along the perforated edges and then to sort them alphabetically, but that is not what the new employee thought he meant.

She had not been employed with Cabela's the last time they had done a mailing, and was therefore unfamiliar with the whole process. Jim carried on with his other responsibilities and assumed his instructions had been clear. You could imagine his surprise when he returned about an hour later to find that the new employee, who was determined to do a good job, was diligently tearing the labels into tiny pieces and throwing them in the wastebasket!

At that time, the company was still struggling and the situation was very serious. Even though the typing had become less arduous after they had discarded the old manual typewriter and bought an electric one, they were nevertheless forced to retype each label to replace the ones she had ripped into pieces and thrown away. Needless to say, the employee made it a point from that time on to make sure she fully understood all instructions.

The new employee had made a mistake, but Dick and Jim were quite understanding. They knew then, and still know now, that mistakes are a part of life, if not an extremely important part of life. If we do not make mistakes, we cannot learn from them. After all, my dad and Jim have made many mistakes with their business but there were never mistakes they could not learn from. I remember overhearing my father telling one of my brothers how important mistakes would be in his life: "It is important to learn from your mistakes if you are to be successful, whether that success is financial or in your personal life. Leading an error-free life is impossible, but the lessons we learn from our mistakes are what help us to survive and grow."

Another reason for the success of Cabela's, which Dad

and Jim often give, is that they have surrounded themselves with top-notch employees. Dad and Jim are both very aware that the company's most important assets are its employees.

When asked to name the two most important reasons for the company's success, Dick did not hesitate at all before he expressed that customer service and talented, well-treated employees were two of the most important factors: "In order to achieve success in the business world you must go one step beyond treating your customers and employees fairly. Respect, honesty and integrity will go a long way, not only in business but in life."

These employees from the early years struggled physically to get the first catalogs out the door. All catalogs were labeled and sorted by state and sacked. They were then loaded into an old green van and taken to the post office just a few blocks down the street. A similar process was repeated when the orders were filled.

The orders for merchandise with the promise of the Cabela's guarantee were continually coming in more steadily and in greater numbers, and all of this was accomplished almost exclusively through word of mouth.

With deep gratitude Dick Cabela explains how he feels about the importance of Cabela's patrons and their recommendations to their friends:

"We gave the consumers quality merchandise at fair prices and assured them that they did not have to keep any item they were not pleased with. And we stood by our promise. Our satisfied customers were the only advertising we had outside of the catalog. In fact, we could not afford any advertising other than the small classified ads in a few of the outdoor publications, and we owe a great deal of our early growth to the kind and generous praise our loyal customers passed on to others."

There were two distinct ways to measure the level of success Cabela's had reached by 1967. Both are obvious valuations of the company's growth and both can be seen before 1967 as well.

Every year realized significant growth for the catalogs and 1967 was no exception. The catalog was over one hundred pages, counting the order blanks, which offered merchandise as well as a place for consumers to fill in their requests.

The 1967 catalog offered more rods, reels and fishing equipment than ever before. It also contained more knives and camping equipment than the preceding catalogs. There were a few new items as well, such as inflatable boats and an entire page of duck and goose calls.

The few items noticeably missing from the catalog were golf equipment and pool tables. Cabela's had finally given up on products their customers had not ordered, creating some of the company's first discontinued items, along with the gimmicky things the housewares flyer had stuck them with.

The necessity of yet another move also served as a testament to their ongoing success. Early in 1967, Dad and Jim made arrangements to trade their current accommodations, the former USDA building, for the Legion Hall building. This site was a bit more spacious and provided for the company's immediate needs. Their growing employee base and expanding inventory had pushed the USDA building beyond capacity.

Sharon Robison remembers Cabela's first move during her time with the company very well:

"Next proved to be a physical move of the company. Cabela's had outgrown their first stand-alone facility. We loaded up and moved the entire thing in a single day. Our new home was the old Legion Hall, a basement building which seemed huge. An elevated area at one end which had been the stage when a band would play at the Legion gatherings, became the new 'office.' The rest of the space was divided into storage of excess merchandise, live picking area, spot for checking and packing orders, a receiving area for new inbound freight, and Cabela's first official retail!

"The front of the Legion Hall building had a wide set of steps leading down into the main part of the building. At the base of these steps we put up a set of tables to work as a barri-cade keeping the customers out of the merchandise-picking area and giving them a hundred square feet or so of space to stand and place their order. Needless to say, it was quite crude, but it worked. Eventually, we had to add on storage space to accommodate the expanding inventory and larger items we began carrying in the catalog. A construction was put on the backside of the building to the alleyway to allow a bit of growth. Also, new personnel were coming on board to handle the increase in orders and requests."

The small retail section was necessary to keep prospec-tive customers from walking through the stocked shelves and bothering the order fillers. The few elongated tables blocked customers from the shelves, but did not deter them from coming in to purchase items.

When a customer came in, one of the employees would become a temporary retail clerk. Normally, when a consumer entered the building, he or she would leaf through a catalog on one of the tables, and show the clerk which item they would like to see. The clerk would then get it from the back.

The clerks soon discovered that if they displayed a few of the more popular items on the tables they could cut down on some of the time spent wandering through the shelves searching for whatever the consumer desired. Cabela's was learning more and more about the retail business every day. Dad and Jim were just starting to formulate their ideas for opening a retail store to better serve their walk-in customers.

The 1967 fall catalog also emphasized the success of the company. Although it had the same number of pages as the previous year, the growth of the catalog was apparent. Fifteen of the thirty-three pages of the 1966 fall catalog were filled with the tried-and-true fishing equipment contained in the profitable spring catalogs. As for the 1967 fall catalog only a single page, the back one, contained fishing equipment, all of which was for ice fishing—a product line which had not been featured in earlier editions.

We could say the 1967 issue was Cabela's first full-fledged fall catalog. It was geared only toward fall and winter outdoor activities such as hunting and ice fishing, and though many of the items in it can be used all year, they are normally associated with the cooler days of fall and winter. Dad and Jim had finally found a solution to the struggles Cabela's experienced during the previous fall and winter seasons.

The brothers loved to fish and hunt and found out through their fall catalog that most of their customers were much like themselves. The relatively few hunting items in the 1966 fall catalog had been accepted by their consumers and had given them the courage and the means to risk much more one year later.

The 1966 fall catalog contained a selection of twelve bows. The number of bows offered in 1967 had risen to twenty-eight. Along with the bigger collection of bows came a larger selection of arrows and other archery equipment, including a good number of broadheads, quivers, and fletching equipment. The catalog had a wider variety of fall and winter clothing, including footwear, gloves, and headgear.

The most prominent items in this fall catalog could also be considered as holding the largest financial risk. Muzzle loading rifles were considered specialty items and therefore required a more substantial investment. There was no guarantee customers would be interested in this product line. Luckily, many of their customers who hunted found ordering these traditional firearms from the catalog more convenient than heading to their local gunsmith.

By studying the catalogs Cabela's distributed in the company's beginning years, we can measure the growth of a business that began in a newspaper ad. From that first ad in the *Casper Tribune* which only produced a single order in 1961

Barbara Tuma-Cabela and James Cabela.

Marian and A.C. Cabela.

Teresa Kerns—Mary Cabela's mother.

Dick and Jim outside their parents' home in Chappell, Nebraska.

Cabela's first headquarters—Dick and Mary's home.

The company's first warehouse—behind Dick and Mary's home.

CABELA DISTRIBUTING

1961

6

BOX 672
CHAPPELL, NEBRASKA

WHOLESALE PRICE LIST

ORDER NOS.	ITEMS	PRICE
217	Hooks---6 hooks to folder. Barbed shank, nylon snelled, hand forged, tied with monofilament nylon, 7" long snells with 3/4" loop. Sizes #4, #6, #8, or # 10. 5 folders (30 hooks)*..	$ .50
231	Hooks---6 hooks to folder. Plain shank, nylon snelled as above. Sizes #4, & #6. 5 folders (30hooks).................	$ .40
228	Leaders---Nylon coated wire leaders with stainless steel snaps. 35 lb. test. Assorted lengths.....................	$ .05 ea.
384	Snaps---Ball bearing swivel snaps. Special friction free design. Brass, nickel plated. Sizes #7 or #10.............	$ .15 doz.
393	Snaps---Ball bearing swivel snaps complete with stainless steel snaps. Packed 7 assorted sizes in plastic box........	$ .15 box
027	Eyelets---No knot eyelet for fly line. A must for every fly fisherman. 2 sizes on a card. Sold everywhere for $ .25..	$ .15 card
046	Flies---Finest quality, grade A, wet or dry hand tied flies. 12 assorted patterns................................	$ .50
041	Flies---Highest quality hand tied flies. 2 flies in a plastic box..	$ .15 box
123	Ketchum---Retail $1.00. Ketchum, the natural fish lure. It attracts fish out of hiding. Try Ketchum and see if your luck doesn't improve.................................	$ .45 Bottle

Cabela's sent this mimeographed sheet to customers who purchased a set of hand-tied flies.

Cabela's first stand-alone building was the old USDA building in Chappell.

CABELA'S
WHOLESALE CATALOG

Fishing Equipment and Supplies

CABELA DISTRIBUTING
Box 547 Chappell, Nebraska

The budding company's first catalog.

Cabela's first security system was Jim's dog Bert.

Dick and Jim traded the old USDA building for the former Legion Hall.

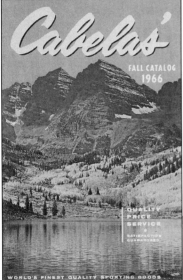

To stimulate sales during fishing's off season Cabela's printed a fall catalog.

The brothers bought this former John Deere building in Sidney, Nebraska for pennies on the dollar. They began drawing salaries that same year.

The company's first official retail was born in Sidney.

Dick and Jim help stock the local pond to give children a place to fish.

Dick and Jim with an outgoing shipment of outdoor goods.

Retail and inbound telemarketing in Kearney, Nebraska.

Cabela's
converted the
old Sioux Army
Depot buildings
into warehouses.

Jim Cabela attempting to land a fish in Alaska.

Flagship catalog showroom was built along Interstate 80 in Sidney.

to two catalogs totaling over 130 pages in 1967, it was apparent that Dick, Mary, and Jim were well on their way to creating a profitable mail-order business that has since attracted a following to the World's Foremost Outfitter that is almost cult-like.

In addition to the growth of the company, my dad and mom had to spend a considerable amount of their time raising their ever-growing family. In September of 1967 they were blessed with another addition to the family—their sixth child, Daniel.

Still working his full-time job at the furniture store, and with six children to raise, it was necessary for Dad to spend odd hours with the young company. Rarely could you find him at the office during normal hours. He would often not make it to the office until the kids were put to bed.

As Sharon Robison recollects, Dick was rarely at the office during normal hours:

"Shortly before we moved the company I noticed a man who made frequent appearances, always having a brief conversation with Jim Cabela and making a swift departure. Finally, I asked who it was and discovered there was a Dick Cabela. Dick and Mary, his wife, put in a multitude of off-site, odd-time hours while Dick maintained his position at the successful Cabela's Furniture Store."

Through hard work, honesty, perseverance and a little luck, Dick, Mary and Jim had found that anything could be accomplished. They had transformed a humble dream and a belief that there were many others who shared their passion for the outdoors into a prosperous and growing business. However, they all knew there was still a long way to go, and when they closed their eyes they began to dream of the possibilities.

$\mathcal{3}$o | *The Move to Sidney*

BY 1968, DICK AND JIM once again realized they needed to expand. The small addition they had previously built onto the Legion Hall couldn't withstand the company's growth. The few people who occasionally entered their buildings over the first few years gave them an insight into the potential for retail sales to supplement the catalogs.

They needed to expand because they had nearly outgrown the Legion Hall and extra space was required for a retail department. As the business continued to mature, the demands upon my dad and my uncle Jim also continued to grow. In 1968 Dad decided to quit the job at his father's furniture store and give full-time attention to the company he had founded and nurtured every spare second he could find between the demands of his job and the demands of his growing family.

Up to this point, Dick and Jim had taken a bit of advice from their father to extremes. They remembered A.C. once explaining to them his simple rule to financial security. He had told his sons, on more than one occasion: "The only way to get ahead in life is to spend less than you make."

That small bit of advice stuck with the two brothers and may have been part of the reason they had been so reluctant to take any of the profits from the company in the first years of business. They both began to draw a salary at this time, but the large majority of the profits still went back into Cabela's Incorporated—they took only what they needed to live.

Chappell is located just off Interstate 80 where the traffic is always steady. The majority of their customers were not local, so Dick and Jim believed a retail store along the Interstate would fare much better than at the downtown location. They purchased about six acres of land just outside of Chappell along the Interstate with the intention of building on the property.

As luck would have it, a man by the name of Chick Cunningham from Sidney, a town about thirty miles west of Chappell, heard a rumor that the Cabela brothers were going to put up a new building near the Interstate. Mr. Cunningham, a real estate broker, contacted my dad and Jim to see if they would be interested in purchasing a building and making a move to Sidney. Dick, Mary and Jim had all attended high school at Saint Patrick's Parochial Academy in

Sidney and were therefore familiar with the community, so they listened with interest.

A John Deere distribution plant in Sidney had closed down and one of their major executives happened to be a former member of the Sidney Hospital Board. This executive convinced the John Deere company to donate the building to the hospital and take the tax write-off. The hospital wanted to transfer ownership of the building before incurring property taxes.

Cabela's, Incorporated was very interested. Sidney's population was about 6,000, and therefore it had a bigger employment base than Chappell, but what clinched the deal was the price. At one dollar per square foot, with no money down, six percent interest, and fifteen years to pay, the deal was far too tempting to pass up. It may not have been as good as three rusty fishhooks for a new puppy, but it was close.

Cabela's purchased the old John Deere building in September of 1968. With a lot of hard work they made the move from Chappell and had the new building occupied and opened early in 1969. Dad and Jim knew they would not put the entire area of the four-story, 50,000-square-foot building to use immediately. The two brothers always looking to the future remembered that the growth they enjoyed in Chappell required moves from Dick and Mary's house, to the basement of their father's furniture store, to the USDA building and finally, the Legion Hall—all in less than eight years. With the size of their new building, they would not need to make another move any time soon.

Of the four stories, only the first floor was needed for business purposes. Everything the growing business required could be done from the first floor including space for offices, fulfilling orders, warehousing, packing and shipping and a small section in the front of the building for retail.

Jack Fuson of Fuson and Associates was amazed when he saw the building Cabela's had purchased:

"When Jim, Mary and Dick moved to their four-story building in Sidney I can remember asking myself what they were going to do with all that open space. As it turned out, it did not take very long for them to outgrow that building."

The remaining floors were put to use shortly after the new building opened. The Cabela's security system moved to Sidney with the company. Burt was allowed to run the entire second floor, which offered plenty of space for him to get all of the exercise he desired. In addition, the top floor was quickly converted into an archery range for Dad, Jim, and the rest of the employees. They recall a few broken windows due to poor shooting. They created the archery range for two purposes— to practice and improve their abilities and to test new products, such as bows and arrows.

The year 1969 proved to be significant for the Cabela family and their employees. Not only did they relocate to Sidney, but in 1969 they also saw sales reach the plateau of one million dollars.

When the retail department in the new building was opened, the new merchandising venture was expected to attract customers from the Nebraska Panhandle, northeastern

Colorado and eastern Wyoming. At the time, that seemed to be a stretch, but by the 1980's, license plates from almost every state could be seen in the Cabela's parking lot throughout the course of one year. When they projected customers from only small areas of three states, their initial predictions were just a tad on the short side.

Toward the end of 1969, their operation had begun to take over parts of the remaining three floors. Burt was once again moved, this time to the third floor during business hours. By 1970, the employees were in the basement to sort labels and affix them to the catalogs. Shipping and retail remained on the first floor until later in the year when shipping had to be moved to the second floor. Large items such as tents were stored on the third floor with Burt.

Dot Kruse, the second person hired from the Sidney area, recalls the terror of venturing to the third floor when one of these items was requested:

"Our burglar alarm was a dog named Burt. He roamed the building at night. During the day he was tied to a post in the center of the third floor. It was a frightening game of wondering if he was tied up or not when you needed to obtain an item from that location. Many was the time that you were part way to your destination and he came tearing to greet you. If you were not frozen in place, there was a mad dash to see if you made it to the door or if you were to become part of his diet for the day."

Merchandise was eventually stored on the second floor. It was a pain to climb the stairs every time a retail customer needed a second-floor item and therefore a hole was cut between the floors. The retail clerks would venture into a back room, look up into the hole and yell out for the requested merchandise. There were several instances when the retail clerk trying to catch the merchandise would miss, and occasionally, the result was a broken item. Without much delay, that system was slightly altered and a nylon net was placed under the hole to do the catching. The net's percentage of goods caught was far better than the often slippery-handed employees'.

Although by 1970 it was apparent the company was doing well, there were still very slow months when it seemed as if the business was really struggling.

Dot Kruse recalls the slow days:

"If I remember accurately there were days when we might have only twenty to thirty orders (100 seemed like a lot!). After the first spring rush was over many of us just knew that we would be laid off. The time cards were kept in a spot directly past Dick and Jim's office. Each day, we were fearful as we walked by to check out that we would be called in and given our notice."

Sharon Robison was astonished when they received more than a few orders in a day:

"During the closing years of the '60's it never failed to amaze me when a quantity of 100 or more orders was received on a single day. It was mind boggling to think that 100 persons had, on the same day, sat down and filled out an order blank, enclosed their payment, affixed a stamp and placed an order with this small mail-order company from small-town Nebraska."

Dad and Jim knew the business was growing and they were still learning along the way. They also recognized that the main reason their company continued to prosper was because their employees were talented, and they needed to keep those employees if they were to continue to grow.

My father and uncle have always downplayed their roles as creators of a world famous mail-order business, contending that most of the credit should be given to their employees and to luck.

Dick and Jim worked extremely hard, but Sharon Robison believes timing also had something to do with the success of the company:

"1961 was an excellent time to start a mail-order business. Today the start-up costs are prohibitive. There are so many companies in the direct-mail business now, that you have to meet the competition head to head with a good looking, expensive catalog just to get noticed."

Even though the company had been doing well for nearly ten years in 1970, Dick and Jim realize many tasks were not handled in the most efficient manner.

Dick explains how changes in technology and customer behavior have affected the company over the years:

"The learning process is never ending. After the first year sales hit the million dollar mark it seemed as if we were doing all the right things. If we were still running things like we were back then, we would not be in business today. You have to be quite flexible and open to change, especially with technology, if you want to compete and survive in the ever changing world of business. With that said, our philosophy has remained the same. It holds as true today as it did in 1961 . . . You have to treat your employees and your customers with honesty and respect, because they will know if you don't."

Some of the inefficient procedures the company had to learn from could be seen in the customer-service department. All the records of a customer's orders were still kept on file cards and filed alphabetically in a small room next door. When a customer called, he or she would be put on hold while the service representative ran over to the area where the cards were kept. While the customer-service representative was frantically searching for the right card, the customer had to wait patiently until the out-of-breath employee returned with the order information.

As inefficient as this sounds, it was not the only problem the customer-service department had to contend with. When Dot Kruse joined the staff in 1972, there were only two phones, one for Sharon Robison and one for the other four staff members. There was no formal employee manual or training for customer service, so they all had no choice but to learn as they went along.

Dot recalls some of the other weaknesses the card system forced them to deal with in the early days:

"Sometimes, during the busy season, the cards would not have been filed back and it would be necessary to go through several stacks to find the card needed. This card only had a record of when the order was received, and the amount of money sent in. If you needed to find the day it was shipped, it was necessary to go through a stack of shipper tags to find this information. If they were misfiled you were in trouble. In addition, this only told you when the order was shipped . . . not what was shipped."

Even though Cabela's Sporting Goods had separate departments, such as customer service and inventory control, all of the employees would do any task necessary. They bound and mailed catalogs, counted beads used on fishing lures, filled orders, packed orders, built shelving, swept the floors and even pitched in once to scrape gum off the floor to prepare it for painting.

Sharon Robison shares a few of the tasks she was responsible for when she first started working for Cabela's:

"It was not unusual for me to check in the received freight, unpack and verify the shipment, place the merchandise on the shelves, open the day's orders, record the method of payment, balance the orders with the receipts, take the orders and pull the merchandise from the shelves, check each order to be certain the proper items were included in the shipment, pack the order, calculate and affix the postage, sort the day's outgoing parcels, take the load to the post office, come back to the office, type in the catalog requests and then clean the bathroom."

Until 1978, the customer-service department handled all complaints and phone orders. Up to that year, phone orders were rare; however, they did get their fair share of customers who would rather call than fill out an order form. The vast majority of these phone orders were paid for with credit cards. Credit cards were just another adaptation for Cabela's. They began accepting them in 1971. The company was strictly a cash only company prior to that year.

The early attempts at credit cards created major problems for the customer-service department. The orders went directly to the credit-card department where the total amount was authorized and charged. The orders were then sent to the shipping department to be filled. Sometimes an item was not in stock and could not be shipped. Since the customer had already been charged for the item, the papers would have to be sent back to the credit-card department so the costs for any items not shipped could be credited back to the consumer's credit card.

If a customer ordered only one item and it was out of stock, nothing was shipped. Therefore, the customer was charged for their order and then credited later. The customer-service representatives had to show extreme patience when these unhappy customers called, primarily to yell at someone.

Cabela's has found that complaints can almost always teach a lesson no matter how small. Customers are not alone with their complaints. Sometimes the business-to-business associates had their own problems, and not always specifically with Cabela's.

Most manufacturers' sales representatives have had great relationships with Cabela's but there were always those few who considered Sidney a hole in the ground way out in the middle of nowhere.

Pat Snyder, Cabela's director of merchandising in the clothing department remembers one sales rep whose first trip to Sidney was his last.

During the early 1980's, Cabela's had begun to grow into a major retailer in the hunting and fishing industry and sales reps started arriving who knew very little about Cabela's, less about the industry and nothing about Sidney. One particular salesman from a manufacturer on the East Coast had a particularly difficult time on his first trip to Sidney, according to Pat Snyder.

It seems that on his forty-five-minute flight to Sidney from Denver, he was seated next to another rep who was more familiar with Cabela's and Sidney. They struck up a conversation and the seasoned rep asked the rookie if he had ever been to Sidney. The novice said he had not.

"So where are you staying tonight," the experienced salesman asked.

"Oh, I'll check into one of the hotels, probably the Marriott."

Little did he know the closest Marriott was back in Denver, and for that matter, Sidney didn't have any national-chain hotels, just locally owned motels. Of course, the seasoned rep didn't inform him of this, but simply laughed to himself and continued questioning. "So how are you going to get into town from the airport?" he asked.

"I'll probably just take a cab," responded the first-time visitor, not knowing the nearest cab was 100 miles from Sidney.

As the plane landed, the pro told the rookie to enjoy his stay in Sidney and, without offering any words of advice, grabbed his bags and was immediately picked up and driven away by the ride he had arranged earlier. He must have been enjoying the fact that his counterpart had no idea of the adventure he was about to embark on.

Back at the airport, the rookie began to realize just how small Sidney was when he asked the only employee there how to call a cab. "We don't have a taxi in Sidney," the airport attendant replied. "But if you look next to the phone, there is a number of a person that will come pick you up if you can get a hold of him." Luckily, the guy was home and agreed to pick up the rep, who was now growing frustrated with the slow-paced small-town atmosphere of Sidney. Shortly, an old beat-up car that to the rep appeared to be a survivor of a demolition derby pulled up outside. The driver got out and a fare was negotiated.

On the short ride to downtown Sidney where Cabela's headquarters was located, and after a history lesson\lecture by the driver, the rookie salesman made up his mind to leave Sidney as soon as possible, which required having a flight rescheduled so he could leave that afternoon rather than the next day.

After he'd completed his business at Cabela's, the story goes, he called his driver who said he would have to take him to the airport immediately because he was busy later in the day when the salesman's flight was scheduled to depart. This left the salesman with four or five hours to burn at the tiny Sidney airport. When he arrived there, the same employee he had talked to earlier told him the airport was closed in the afternoon, since only two flights arrived per day, and that his options were to come back in four or five hours or be locked in the airport until the employee returned to process the evening flight. He chose the latter. Obviously he was ready to get out of town and was not going to chance getting stuck in Sidney overnight. His adventure was soon relayed to his peers in the industry and Pat Snyder recalls that this salesman never made another visit to Sidney.

Cabela's customer service is second to none and even during those times when dealing with customer orders seemed to be as inefficient as possible the friendly personalities of the customer-service representatives would shine through. No matter how frustrated a customer would get the customer-service representatives would do their very best to help and were always polite and courteous.

Dick and Jim were genuinely upset when customers were not completely satisfied with the products or the service. This concern has not changed at Cabela's today. Cabela's has gone out of its way to try to make each customer happy. That was, and still is, their goal. Sometimes that goal is impossible and some customers will never be completely satisfied, but it is a great feeling for Dick and Jim to know that nearly all of Cabela's customers keep coming back because they are one hundred percent satisfied.

Customer loyalty is not what it used to be in any industry, but at Cabela's it is like that of a champion bird dog to its human hunting companion. Many of the products Cabela's offers can be bought elsewhere, but customers keep coming back to do business with Cabela's. Dick gives the credit of this phenomenon to the history of the company's exceptional customer service:

"When customers shop at Cabela's and are one hundred percent satisfied, we can not only expect them to return, but we can also expect them to tell their friends. When you treat people well, you would be amazed at how quickly word gets out. There really is no better advertising than that of a satisfied customer."

By 1973, the new building was almost full. After only five years in Sidney, the 50,000-square-foot building was nearly at maximum capacity. The growth came from all departments of the company: retail, inventory, office space, shipping and packing had all developed to the point where Cabela's was too big for the building which at the time of purchase Dad and Jim thought would last much longer than five years. They sure are glad it didn't.

Five years had been the longest they had stayed in one building since my father had purchased those hand-tied flies in 1961. They had become somewhat attached the old John Deere building and were tired of moving. They had no intention of leaving the Sidney area, and moving the headquarters to another building was just not feasible at the time.

So they decided their best bet would be to purchase another building. All they needed was a warehouse. If they could move most of the inventory to a nearby warehouse, the offices and the shipping and packaging departments could remain in the current building.

As it turned out, they had an opportunity to purchase the building next door. It was approximately 14,000 square feet and would be perfect for warehousing. The brothers were most certain the extra space would be more than sufficient for some time to come.

While the rest of the company was flourishing and changing, the old recipe-card file system still remained intact. Employees could always tell which customers were new and which had been buyers for years, just by looking at the conditions of the customer cards.

Sharon Robison explains how the card system was set up when she first started with Cabela's in 1965:

"All of our customer information was kept in a shoe box on recipe cards. You could tell which customers were new— their cards were sharp-edged and clean . . . the old customer cards were grimy . . . the multiple purchase customers were dog-eared. The direct marketing industry at the turn of the century is consumed with maintaining customer records in a database which can be examined to study historical evidence and create predictive models. Millions of pieces of information can be put to cartridges and Cabela's total customer records would once again fit in a shoe box. I guess this is a matter of technology coming full circle."

The inefficient card-file system was finally put to rest around 1975. Technology was just beginning to catch up with Cabela's and they decided to put in a computer system. As hard as it was to get rid of the card-file system, they somehow made the transition. That is not to say the computer system did not have complications and inefficiencies of its own. Anyone who owns a computer understands that problems and glitches are all too common. Just try to imagine those encountered in 1975.

When the Customer-Service Department received their first computer terminal they found that sometimes the new system was just as inefficient as the card-file system. For a while, the five customer-service representatives had to share one computer terminal. Very seldom did just one customer call in at a time. Calls were continuously coming in, and because they had only a single terminal, the representatives were forced to stand in line while their respectful customers waited patiently on the phone until it was their representative's turn.

To make matters worse, the computer system at that time was only capable of supplying the date of the customer's order and the amount of the order. The only way the representatives could find anything out about what product they had ordered was to have the customer explain it to them.

On the surface this may not appear to be good customer service at all, but the fact that Cabela's customers kept coming back disputes that assumption. It is quite true the customer-service representatives had to work extra hard at times to satisfy some of them, but they were all great with people, an enormous asset to the company in those learning years.

The early seventies also brought our family its final three

children: Carolyn was born in 1971; David (yours truly) in 1972; and Joseph in 1974. With nine growing children to attend to every day, it is amazing our parents had time to build a world-renowned outdoor sporting goods company. Mary and Dick believe their lives would not have been complete without each and every one of their nine children.

Toward the end of the 1970's, Cabela's had, once again, outgrown their facilities. The main area of concern was the warehouse facility. As the company's customer base grew, so grew the inventory, and within six years the 14,000-square-foot warehouse was no longer capable of meeting the demands of the ever expanding direct-mail-order company.

Located ten miles northwest of Sidney, the former Sioux Army Depot consisted of some aging buildings once used for storing ammunition and military equipment. The facilities had been vacant for some time and most were in need of repair work, especially on the roofs.

Despite the distance, Dad and Jim believed the 90,000 square feet of each building would be ideal for the pace at which they were growing. They bought one of the buildings, did a little renovating, replaced the worn-out roof and moved the bulk of their warehousing to the new site.

The purchase of this first building provided enough space only until 1983. However, the old depot building proved to be beneficial, prompting the brothers to purchase two more of the buildings. In addition, they built on a 30,000-square-foot break room which connected two of the buildings. The total of 300,000 square feet was quite a jump from that first warehouse behind Mom and Dad's home in Chappell.

One of the buildings was quickly converted for shipping, receiving and long-term storage. Then, in the summer of 1984, warehousing was made more uniform when all merchandise on the second floor was moved from town to the warehouse location. The warehouses served as more than just space for storage. Merchandise was also received, packed and mailed to customers from these facilities.

All merchandise was initially sent to Receivings by truck or UPS. It was separated by manufacturer, counted, tagged, and sorted by destination. Exact numbers needed for back orders and store stock were pulled and sent to the appropriate warehouse.

After Receiving was put online with the mainframe computer, updates on purchase orders and inventory count were automatic and immediate. Once an order had been keyed in by computer, it was printed on a picking slip. Orders were hand pulled directly from summary labels and sent to the packing tables by way of conveyor belts. Here they were sealed and weighed, then loaded directly into UPS Drop Shipment trailers for transport.

Today, automation plays a vital role in the processing of an order. The movement of paperwork and merchandise through the fulfillment area is a symphony in motion as orders pass through the conveyor system. Information is now read with scanning equipment and parcels are handled a minimal number of times by human hands. Due to the nature of Cabela's inventory, automated picking is not possible. There are simply too many small items to make it practical. Trucks pull up to the fulfillment building and loads are directly dropped to several locations within the United States.

After these warehouses were operational, Dad used to visit the facilities quite frequently. Some say he did so more to hunt pheasants than to check on the warehousing operations.

Dick himself does not completely deny those accusations:

"I used to love going out to the warehouses, it gave me an excuse to do some pheasant hunting during the season. I used to put my shotgun in the back seat of the car before leaving the offices. After you got out of town the drive to the warehouses was mostly done on gravel country roads. There were a couple of really nice fields on the way that were great for pheasants. Almost everyone in the Panhandle of Nebraska is hospitable and friendly making it quite easy to gain permission to hunt on the local farmer's land. I always wondered what some of the passers-by must have thought when they saw a man in a business suit walking in a field carrying a shotgun."

Usually somebody out at the warehouses knew my father was coming, whether it was just to check up on the operations or to meet specifically with an individual or group. When he said he was on his way, they knew he would be a little longer than expected if the hunting was good.

4. From a Passion to a Business

What Do They Know?

Like anyone who hunts or fishes a lot, Jim and I have had our share of discouraging experiences with guides.

When Jim and I were fishing on Sam Rayburn Lake in Texas, our guide insisted on cruising up the lake, checking all the points for schooling bass. All he was interested in was a quick limit of small, schooling bass so he could limit us out by noon and call it a day.

Soon, Jim and I had enough. I told the guide that Jim and I could catch small bass back home. The guide agreed and let us choose the water we wanted to fish. We told him to stop and anchor at the mouth of a small creek that emptied into the river channel. We checked the depth and it was perfect, dropping off from four to twenty feet.

The time was 11:30. I told Jim that when I lived on Lake of the Ozarks, I caught all my large bass at noon. Jim made several casts to the drop-off and caught three nice bass. From that time on, the guide was more cooperative.

That evening, at the fish cleaning table, I overheard another guide ask our guide if the Cabela's people knew what they were talking about. Our guide responded, 'You can bet your ass they do.'

—J.E. "Buster" Coffey

A history of Cabela's would not be complete without a few words about the passion, shared by millions, including Dick, Mary and Jim, that has truly made Cabela's a success. You would be hard pressed to find a hunter or angler in the United States who has not heard of Cabela's. Most outdoor enthusiasts are almost as passionate about their equipment as they are about their hunting, fishing, and camping, and one of their favorite places to buy that equipment is Cabela's.

You may even be hard pressed to find a hunter or angler anywhere in the world who has not at least heard of Cabela's.

Cabela's currently fills orders from more than 130 countries. Once again, the common bond that brings all of these customers to Cabela's is their unparalleled passion for the outdoors.

Even Dick was unaware of just how many people in different countries had heard of Cabela's—until one time when he was on an overseas trip:

"I remember when we received our first foreign order. It was amazing to think someone from another country had heard of Cabela's. A few years ago Mary and I were in New Delhi, India. We had purchased some local art and I presented my credit card for payment. The man behind the desk broke into a wide, toothy grin and shouted, 'I know you!! I know you!!' I'd never seen the man in my life, but after a couple of minutes of conversation, I discovered he was a Cabela's customer. It was at that point that I realized we had earned our title, World's Foremost Outfitter."

The fact Cabela's has become a globally known corporation is truly amazing when you consider that the business started out as a kitchen-table hobby. It has helped that the Cabela brothers know exactly who their customers are. All they have to do is look in the mirror.

The Cabelas have surrounded themselves with people who love the outdoors just as passionately as they do. This mutual bond shared by Dick, Mary, Jim, Cabela's employees, and Cabela's customers, is the pumping heart that has kept Cabela's healthy and growing and has given them an edge.

The diverse group that encompasses the hunting and

fishing world has allowed Cabela's to stay away from the demographic information that many mass direct-marketing companies purchase. Cabela's only needs a snapshot of each of their customers, so that they might know how a customer will react to each new mailing.

The Cabela brothers believe in their own privacy and therefore believe in the privacy of their customers. The company only keeps basic information about a customer, such as address, home and work phone numbers, the number of orders, and dollar amount for each, the types of merchandise ordered, the number of catalogs sent, credit history, and merchandise returned and replaced. This data is used only for company purposes and is not released to other mailers.

A common practice among direct-marketing companies is to purchase extra information on individuals to overlay their customer records. Cabela's has found that this appended data is not of much value to them. Dick explains why:

"Our customers are dedicated outdoor enthusiasts and are described best by lifestyle rather than by a set of demographics. At a small stream you may find two persons side by side. One drove his Land Rover, the other his twenty-year-old Chevy pickup; one has a lunch of boiled eggs, the other a jar of Beluga caviar, but both are Cabela's customers and have spent an equal amount on their fishing equipment. Their common bond is the fact that they love to go fishing."

Those who take part in outdoor conservation activities such as hunting and fishing are an extremely diverse family of individuals. Participation in the undeniable cycle of life is not limited to any age, sex or race.

I remember one recent year when I headed to the Lincoln, Nebraska Game and Parks office to pick up a deer permit. In Nebraska there is a lottery for deer permits and any remaining after the lottery are sold on a first-come-first-serve basis. On the first day they went up for sale after the lottery, I took the morning off and drove to the office, thinking I could pick one up and get back home in time for an early lunch.

When I arrived at the Game and Parks facility I was amazed by the long line of fellow deer hunters waiting patiently, in the hope there would still be licenses left for them when they reached the front of the line. There were more than two hundred people in line when I showed up and it had shrunk by at least half since the office opened that Monday morning. The encouraging thing about this line was that the majority of the people waiting were smiling, laughing and conversing with strangers. Most of them were sharing their personal experiences of time spent in the outdoors.

The point of the story is that of those two hundred-plus hunters waiting in line, about twenty to twenty-five percent were women and at least fifteen percent were members of minority groups. There were also children in the line who were no older than twelve or thirteen and there were senior citizens over ninety.

This diversity of wildlife lovers who hunt is only one small example from Lincoln, Nebraska. Just think how diverse the hunting population is, taking into account the whole nation, or better yet the entire world. There are hunters and anglers in every corner of the globe who share a this love for wildlife and all its beauty.

Hunting and angling tend to get bad raps from some media and anti-hunting groups who often see hunting and fishing as the mindless slaughter of defenseless animals. Entrenched opinions based on well-intentioned emotional perceptions are difficult to sway, but an open-minded discussion of the scientific facts and some quality time dropping a nymph into a stream or leisurely working a dog in a CRP field may allow them to rethink their logic.

Long before it became fashionable to call yourself an environmentalist, hunters and anglers were pouring time and money into conservation. They were the first environmentalists, and they understood and became a part of the natural cycle of life encompassing the wilderness around them.

Hunters and anglers have given more back to wildlife and wilderness habitat than any other group of people or organization. They know they are consumptive users of wildlife and long to do their part to give back to nature. One of the ways hunters and anglers give back is through the billions of dollars they give through contributions, purchasing permits, and excise taxes. In fact, over eighty cents of every dollar spent on conservation comes from the pockets of hunters and anglers.

Dick, Mary and Jim Cabela have given more than their share of funds to help conservation efforts and they do not regret a single penny. Their love for wildlife is far too strong for them not to do more than their fair share.

Dick explains how all hunters and anglers choose to give something back to nature:

"It seems like every time you turn around these days, someone is trying to take away the thing sportsmen hold most dear—the legacy of America's outdoor sports. Fact is, our strong outdoor heritage continues today, and will continue for years to come, because of sportsmen. With voluntary contributions, self-imposed excise taxes and conservation organizations, America's sportsmen have led the way in game management and habitat improvement."

My father was speaking of self-imposed excise taxes outdoor participants pay and the laws hunters and anglers have pushed into being passed which ensure that all hunters and anglers help fund efforts to conserve wildlife. Most of these self-imposed taxes were put into effect before it was politically correct to say you cared about the environment. Here are a few examples:

PITTMAN-ROBERTSON ACT—Passed in 1937, ensures that an eleven percent tax on rifles, shotguns, ammunition, and archery equipment used for hunting goes to further wildlife conservation.

SPORT FISH RESTORATION ACT—Since 1950, has mandated a ten percent manufacturer's excise tax on fishing rods, reels, creels, artificial baits, lures and flies, with revenue earmarked solely for projects to enhance sport-fishing restoration.

WALLOP-BREAUX TAX—Introduced in 1984, extends the Sport Fish Restoration Act tax to include tackle boxes and other recreational equipment. Also channels import duties on fishing tackle and pleasure boats into fisheries restoration.

FEDERAL DUCK STAMPS—More than 350 million dollars from the sale of duck stamps have gone to preserve almost four million acres of wetland refuges for North American waterfowl. Since 1934, every waterfowl hunter sixteen years of age or older has been required to purchase and carry an annual stamp.

America can thank its hunters and anglers for the ever increasing numbers of wildlife we enjoy today. In the 1920's pronghorn antelope numbers had fallen to fewer than 25,000; today there are around 800,000. White-tailed deer have increased from a low of 500,000 animals in the 1920's to more than 14,000,000 today. Many more success stories like these may be attributed to American hunters and anglers.

Some anti-hunting advocates say conservationists only try to increase the population of game animals so they can kill more of them. Nothing could be further from the truth.

Consider a species that will never be hunted—the bald eagle. This is a tremendous success story for the recovery of a species that can be directly attributed to the dollars and efforts of hunters and anglers.

At one point it was discovered that the decline of the bald eagle and other raptors was largely due to the use of insecticides on croplands which were poisoning the birds. The dollars that funded the research that led to this discovery came directly and indirectly from hunters and anglers. Furthermore, the four million acres of wildlife refuges provided by money from Federal Duck Stamps are used for nesting and breeding grounds by bald eagles.

Hunters who are fortunate enough to have land of their own spend countless dollars for habitat restoration, which benefits not only game animals and bald eagles, but many species of animals which they know will never be hunted. No group or organization has given more to the conservation efforts of game and non-game animals and fish than have hunters and anglers. None have even come close. Hunters and anglers are solely responsible for nearly all conservation.

Dick and Jim Cabela understand and appreciate these efforts and would like to give their thanks:

"The results of sportsmen's efforts have been dramatic, benefiting non-game animals as well as people who like to hike, camp, watch birds, and photograph wildlife. It is mostly the unnoticed efforts of the American sportsmen and women doing their part as responsible conservationists that will determine the future of our nation's wildlife. And for these efforts, we at Cabela's say thank you to the American sportsmen and sportswomen."

Dad, Mom and Jim never really knew how far this kitchen-table hobby would take them. My dad always wanted to start a business of his own but he never knew that the years of hard work and sticking with it, even when it appeared hopeless, would reward him with a hunter's dream.

My parents began traveling to Africa to hunt big game in 1987 and have been going back almost every year since. Many hunters dream of venturing to the Dark Continent to experience the grandeur of one of the world's two most famous wildlife arenas, the other being North America. Through hard work and perseverance, Dick, Mary and Jim have made this dream a reality.

Since their first trip to Africa, my parents have traveled and hunted in many parts of the world, but my father believes, the untamed lands in Africa are special:

"Mary and I fell in love with Africa from the very beginning. It's hard to explain unless you have experienced it, but it gets into your blood. We finally understood why Hemingway always returned to Africa. The only way to truly understand is to experience Africa for yourself."

A large part of the African lure is its wilderness. Hunters and anglers understand that the human species is inherently wild. Although many people have forgotten their natural instincts, they are still remembered by hunters and anglers in every part of the world.

To the hunter, angler and conservationist, wild places are

more than a weekend destination or temporary getaway. The reason hunters and anglers go to such great lengths to protect the wilderness at their own expense is because they do not think of other living things as separate from themselves. When a hunter goes into the wilderness, he or she is really just going home.

Dick, Mary and Jim enjoy hunting and fishing in the same mountains, plains, deserts, oceans, lakes and streams as their average customer does. They still hunt and fish in those familiar places, but they also enjoy exploring and experiencing new places.

Dad and Jim realized early that hiring outdoor enthusiasts as employees would result in better understanding of their customer needs. They do not expect all of their employees to love the outdoors but they do encourage outdoor experiences. They know the rewards and blessings the outdoors has to offer and the employees who experience the awesome wild places know just how important each Cabela's customer is, not only for the company, but for the continued success of conservation efforts.

One of the positions most coveted at Cabela's is that of the Product Specialist. These associates are experts in the field of outdoor products. They are required to prove their knowledge in test form. Many individuals have to take the Product Specialist test a few times before they pass it. The test is quite difficult and those who can pass it have almost exclusively acquired their knowledge by using outdoor products directly in the field. All of the associates at Cabela's are knowledgeable about the products, but the Product Specialists are truly experts.

Dick, Mary and Jim have taken a love for the outdoors and combined it with a lot of hard work, turning it into one of the best known, best liked outdoor outfitting companies in the world. They have found their own passions are not all that different from those of millions of other men and women throughout the world who have chosen not to suppress their natural instincts.

Despite all the success the brothers have had, they have not forgotten the humble nature of their small-town upbringing nor lost their love for all living things, inspired by their lives in the natural world. They have found that true freedom can be found in the wild places and understand the important role their customers play in preserving this wilderness they call home.

Those who have spent time with Jim, Dick and Mary in the outdoors have seen them at their best, when they are truly at ease. Some of the sales representatives, employees and colleagues who have shared hunting and fishing experiences with the Cabelas have become great friends and were kind enough to share a few of their memories:

Lifelong Friend

In 1980, just four months after starting at Cabela's, I was living a dream come true. At 5 p.m. on a Friday, Jim Cabela and I were heading down the road to fish for a long weekend at

Lake Powell. With plans made, groceries bought, tackle organized and $25 in my pocket, I was pumped.

The sun set quickly on our nine-hour drive, but I had no problem staying awake and jabbering enough to keep Jim awake. When we finally pulled up at the lake in Jim's old green Blazer (he wasn't much for new vehicles in those days), it was obviously time to crash for a few hours.

By 6 a.m. we were heading toward the marina to pick up our rental boat. Soon the gear was packed into the 16-foot boat and we were cruising down the lake.

Jim captained the boat. I stacked a couple of jackets across a pile of gear in front and lay back facing the stern of the boat with my feet up on a cooler. Ah, this is life—the president of Cabela's motoring me to my fishing spot. The only other boat on the water was a 20-foot tri-hull filled with parents, kids and water toys angling the same direction we were.

As they closed the distance between us, I had the feeling they didn't know we were there. I shouted at Jim and pointed behind him. Realizing he couldn't hear me over the motor, I yelled a little louder. 'Jim!' It was too late. I jumped up in the front of the boat, frantically waved my hat over my head and yelled, 'hey!' Jim looked back over his right shoulder in time to see the bow of the boat coming over him. Instinctively, he thrust the tiller handle away, spinning us to the right. The driver of the tri-hull finally saw me over the inflatable toys and cranked his wheel just as his hull came over Jim. The keel crashed through our motor cowling and transom. With our motor acting like a ski jump, the big tri-hull did a 007-style flight and side-skidded to a stop. Amazingly, nobody was hurt and there was minimal damage to both boats. After gathering ourselves, we exchanged names, insurance information and a few choice words and gimped back to the marina.

Soon we were off again with another new rental knowing we had just missed the best part of the fishing day. We stopped at the first 'fish'-looking spot we saw and it took just three casts to start our next adventure.

Out from the steep canyon wall we were fishing came a snake swimming right for our boat. Jim spurted out some Latin sub-species lingo and wanted to catch it to get a closer look. I, not knowing anything about western snakes, wanted it dead. Without much conversation, Jim scooped it up in the landing net. I, without saying anything, whipped out my fillet knife and before the net cleared the gunwale, made a swift swing at the snake's head—only to cleanly slice the bottom third of Jim's trout net off. Jim looked at me, I looked at Jim, Jim looked at the snake, which now was swimming unscathed toward shore. With a red face, I sheepishly muttered out a few dozen apologies as Jim patiently got a roll of decoy cord out of his bag and began mending the net.

We fished the rest of the morning until Jim suggested we take a break and set up camp. Straight ahead of us was a large, flat, rock island in the middle of a bay. It was probably 15 feet above the water level, had a low end we could climb to get on top and was quite unique. After camp was set and we had lunch, Jim decided to rig up his fly rod for some pan-fishing fun.

Jim always had top-notch equipment. That day, he had a Cabela's Fish Eagle rod and a beautiful Hardy fly reel. Anxious to feel the reel, I picked it up, spun the handle and pulled the line against the drag. What happened next, I cannot explain. All I know is the English-made heirloom was falling in slow-motion towards the huge cement-like rock we were standing on. With cat-like reflexes, I thrust my right foot forward so my boot could cushion the reel's fall.

In four years of high school football, I never once connected like I did that afternoon. As Jim and I watched the reel skid, flip and scrape across that rock surface, our only hope was that it would stop before it got to the water. The good news was the water was only about 15 feet deep. After my quick bath, we headed back out on our quest, caught several nice fish and returned to camp that evening.

With a ferocious wind storm that night, another long day of fishing and a drive home the next day through torrential rain, the rest of the trip was just as eventful as the first day. When Jim dropped me off at my apartment, I knew that after a weekend like this, I would either be fired the next day or I had just made a life-long friend.

—Tom Rosdail Senior
Merchandise Manager
Fishing/Marine

Stuck Between A Hard Place And An Elephant

One memory which sticks out in my mind was an experience I shared with my mother on a trip I took to Zambia with my parents. We awoke one morning about 3:30 in search of Chobi bushbuck.

We were traveling in a Toyota Land cruiser and our guide suggested that he, my mother and I should ride up on top where we would have a better view. The head tracker was the only one left who could drive the vehicle and was very inexperienced.

We were going along pretty good when a group of elephants suddenly appeared to the right. In an excited tone our guide warned his head tracker to slow down quickly. The elephants were too close!

Once the elephants began to go about their way our guide said we could speed back up. As soon as we started to speed up our inexperienced driver stalled the vehicle. Before he could get the engine to jump back to life an elephant cow came in from the left side.

We were stuck between a cow elephant that wanted to get back to her group and four other elephants which wanted her to be back in their group, and us tiny humans were the only things in the way. Our guide was yelling nervously for Mom to shoot her rifle into the air. One minor problem—Mom's gun was still down in front. The tension was very high.

The rising agitation the elephants were displaying added to our nervousness.

When Mom finally got her gun she was so rattled she loaded and unloaded it twice. She finally fired the rifle and at about the same time the driver got the vehicle moving. The elephants were reunited and we were safely on our way but not without an excited memory that would last forever.

—Teri Wolff

(Mary and Dick's daughter)

Mexican Mahi Mahi

When I was ten years old we went to Loreto, Mexico to go fishing for Mahi Mahi. We had two guides and two teensy weensy boats (about ten feet in length). We couldn't all fit in one, so Dad, Dave and Joe went in one boat and Mom and I went in another.

It was extremely hot and we were in what seemed like the middle of the ocean fishing. I hooked a fish and after fifteen minutes of struggling with it I was exhausted! I thought it was never going to reach the boat. Mom took over and after another thirty minutes or so she got it up to the boat. It was a huge Mahi Mahi (over six ft. long) and beautiful. You could see all the colors of the rainbow on its side.

I think the guide shot it with a gun and at that point it turned into the blackest ugliest fish I had ever seen! It immediately lost all of its color. It was pretty strange. It was very exciting to be so young and to catch a fish of this magnitude.

Soon after the catch, a shark came swimming by our boat. It was much bigger than our boat and I was scared half to death! The shark just kept circling around the boat. I am sure it smelled (or whatever fish do) the blood from the Mahi Mahi we just killed, but I was sure it was there to kill us! Dad was far away . . . Mom was freaking out as well and our guide spoke no English!

All in all it was a lot of excitement in one day for a child my age. It didn't stop there, either. After the shark left and we went back to the shore, we were told that the Mahi Mahi would have been a record for that year. We then were able to take the fish to the hotel restaurant where they cooked it for our dinner. Dave, Joe and I hated fish, so we weren't too happy about it, but much to our surprise the fish tasted awesome. The first time I ever actually enjoyed fish.

My first time deep sea fishing I catch a huge Mahi Mahi, have a shark circle our ten foot

boat and enjoy the taste of fish for the first
time . . . what a great experience for a young
child. It is definitely one of my favorite childhood memories!

—Carolyn Harvey
(Mary and Dick's daughter)

Bugling Elk

After a hard day of archery elk hunting with
Rick Bouldin, Jim, and Dick Cabela, we were
all relaxing in our tent. We had hunted very
hard all day and had not seen nor heard one
single elk. Our spirits were down a bit but we
still had hope. Then, just as we were finishing
dinner we heard an elk bugling in the distance.
We were all filled with excitement and anticipation of what tomorrow might bring. As we
began a serious discussion on our hunting
strategies for the following day, Dick started
laughing. Being the trickster that he was, he
had placed a tape recorder mimicking elk
bugles in the bushes behind our tent.
Although a bit disappointed that the bugle
wasn't true, we all had a good laugh.

—Mike Wieser
Divisional Merchandise Manager
Hunting/Optics/Outdoor

Overtime

In 1990, Cabela's was considering taking on a line of fishing boats and pontoons. Being the responsible company that Cabela's is, it was deemed necessary to test this product before presenting it to our customers. Several product specialists, product managers and Jim Cabela took one of the pontoons to Lake McConaughy on a workday afternoon for a test drive. After several hours of cruising and fishing, someone's watch alarm signaled that it was 5 p.m. Jim looked at his watch and said, "Do you guys mind if we put in a little overtime tonight?" Of course, we agreed that, for the betterment of the company, we could all stay a little while longer.

—Rick Trollier
Quality Control Manager

Halibut Fishing for Whale

We were fishing for halibut and salmon off the coast of Alaska and on this particular day the fishing was going pretty slow. We had been catching plenty of smaller halibut the previous few days and decided to go after a bigger fish. After a couple of hours without a nibble my brother, David, and I began to get restless.

Mom was starting to doze off so we decided to have a little fun with her. From two different angles behind her we reached our poles over at the same time and touched her hair lightly. At first, she just waved her hand above her head without opening her eyes. The next time we messed with her hair with more enthusiasm and received the reaction we desired. She almost jumped into the water screaming and swatting at her hair. "That's not funny," she said glaring at us as we turned red with laughter.

Our little prank only kept us alert for a few minutes. Before long, Mom was starting to doze off again—I think the fish must have been sleeping as well. Right after our guide told us to reel in so we could go to a different spot, Dad's line took off and his reel began to scream. Dad reached for his rod as smoke started drifting from the reel. Almost everyone was excited by the sudden explosion in the action. As we all hollered 'fish on!' our guide jumped from his seat and cursed, 'Damn, you hooked a whale.' Immediately after our guide cut the line, a huge anchor-shaped tail rose out of the water and waved, as if to say, 'Goodbye, thanks for the laugh. You should have seen the look on your faces.'

—Joe Cabela

Exploding Reel

One of my most memorable fishing trips was when Jim Cabela and I went to Coiba Island, Panama. Coiba was the site of Panama's 'Alcatraz' and with the exception of the guides, all of the camp's personnel were inmates, some lifers. The fabulous fishing quickly made us forget our nervousness. One day we were trolling four lines from our Mako and we ran into a school of yellow fin tuna. All four reels screamed at once. Jim, the guide and myself each grabbed a rod. The fourth reel continued to whine, smoke and then explode, startling us for a moment. I had never experienced that before nor have I seen it since.

—J.B. Jorgenson
Sales Rep

Roof-Top Pigeon Shoots

When Cabela's entered the premium shotgun business in 1987, we assumed we would have to accept some trade-ins, but nobody really knew what to expect. So when a customer sent in a beautiful old L.C. Smith Crown-Grade shotgun as trade for a Merkel, I was not sure how to proceed. When Jim came in with the daily stack of 'fan mail,' I showed him the gun and asked what he thought. Of Course, his first question was, 'what's wrong with it?' not believing someone would want to trade a beautiful Crown-Grade Smith for a Merkel.

I told Jim that I could not find anything wrong under initial inspection, but was going to run out to his farm and shoot a few rounds through it to see what would happen. Jim got his famous grin on his face and said, 'Why wait?'

He grabbed the gun, I dug up some shells and up on the roof we went gathering Dennis Highby and a few others along the way. The gun was put to the test on the numerous pigeons that made their home on top of Cabela's three-story World Headquarters. The gun worked admirably, and our trade-in testing procedure was established.

Over the next few weeks, we received more trade-ins that required testing. A strict code of conduct was established: Never shoot over the parking lot; only shoot pigeons directly over the roof; and never shoot more than a couple of rounds at a time. Everything worked great until Jim attempted a double on a flock that had caught a thermal coming up the building. The first bird hit the roof perfectly, but the second bird fell like a rock right next to a customer going into the store.

The startled customer went about shopping, never learning what caused that pigeon to suddenly die in mid-flight. But the director of Human Resources immediately had an idea what had happened. He came running up the back stairs hoping to catch me and some of the other buyers in the act. Imagine his chagrin when the first two people he met were Jim and Dennis Highby running down the stairs. Of course, Dennis had handed me the gun and shells, so I still caught some heat over the ordeal. Needless to say, we developed a different procedure to test trade-ins.

—Fred Neal
Divisional Merchandise Manager
Fishing/Marine

Pheasant Hunting Business

While I had the Cabela's account from 1968 to 1975, I had the pleasure of spending several days fishing with Jim on Lake McConaughy. I cannot remember if we caught many fish, but I always enjoyed Jim's company on these trips.

On one occasion, I also had the honor of going pheasant hunting with Jim, Dick, and

Mary. I had called Jim from Grand Island, Nebraska, to confirm our meeting the next day. He asked me if I had my hunting gear, which I did, and he asked me to meet him, Dick and Mary at a local restaurant in Sidney at 6 a.m.

I was happy with the invitation, but I hated to lose the morning as my original thoughts were to spend the morning writing orders. I met the hunting party at the restaurant for breakfast and then we headed out hunting.

After a few hours of hunting, Jim and I went in for lunch and then to the office. Jim went to his desk, picked up some papers, handed them to me and told me to quit worrying about the time lost hunting. Jim had written all the orders the night before! This was just one of the courtesies given to me during the years I worked with Cabela's.

During my many years as a manufacturer's representative, I called on many fine accounts, but none more pleasurable than Jim and Dick Cabela. The thing that impresses me most is the fact they are still the same wonderful family they were when I made my first call at Cabela's.

—Ken Carter
Sales Rep

Flying Dessert

In 1973, Jim Cabela, Rick Bouldin and I headed for Glenwood Springs, Colorado for our first elk hunt. Jim was to be the camp chef and we decided freeze-dried food would be the easiest choice. Most of it was edible, with the exception of a blueberry cobbler dessert Jim had prepared one evening. At first, Rick and I tried to force it down, but this was impossible. We acted as if we were enjoying it, but when Jim was not looking, we would fling spoonfuls of it over our shoulders. Within minutes, we had a large flock of jays taking over our camp-site enjoying the cobbler much more than us. I still don't know if Jim ever realized what caused all of those birds to suddenly show up.

—Mike Wieser
Divisional Merchandise Manager
Hunting/Optics/Outdoor

Fish On

My 30+ years of calling on Cabela's has been full of interesting experiences, with many laughs and lots of good humor. In the early 1970's, while on a visit to the Gerber Knife factory, Jim, Dick, Mary and I went salmon fishing in the Pacific. I held my rod while everyone else left theirs in the rod holders. All the rods were hooking fish except for mine, it was absolutely humiliating. I wanted to be ready to hook the fish if I got a bite while they just let the fish hook themselves, and caught all the fish. Just as I would start concentrating really hard Mary would sneak up behind me and jerk the rod butt. I don't remember if I ever caught a fish that day but we sure had a lot of fun.

—Tom Lewis
Sales Rep

Fishing Prodigy

Shortly after I started working at Cabela's in 1985, spring arrived and everyone began to catch the fishing bug. Several of us planned a family fishing and camping trip to Glendo Reservoir in Wyoming.

I have two sons, Karl and Justin, who at the time were about 8 and 12 years old. They already loved to fish and hunt and thought that every day would be Christmas after I started working at Cabela's. To top it off, we would be fishing with Jim Cabela on that trip.

After arriving at Glendo and setting up camp, we set out to do some fishing. That first day, the fishing was pretty slow until late in the afternoon. We were drifting in the back of Muddy Bay and I think everyone was in the process of changing lures in the hopes of catching a fish when Karl caught a walleye while drifting a crawler rig.

We all changed baits quickly to get into the action. Every time we would make a drift, Karl would catch a fish. Jim, Justin and myself never caught a fish, yet Karl would catch one every drift. Jim kept laughing and saying, "Way to go, Karl." It got to the point where all we could do was laugh at the fact that Karl's crawler was the only one the fish were interested in, no matter where he sat in the boat.

That evening we had fresh walleye and a great time around the campfire with Jim still laughing and talking about Karl catching all the fish. It was a great trip with some wonderful people.

I don't suppose it's been Christmas every day for the past 15 years, but it sure has been great and I have enjoyed many memorable experiences and lots of good times with the Cabela's family.

—Bob Pickard
Returns Supervisor
Oshkosh

Annual Fish Meeting

The annual sales meeting with our major manufacturers required a trip to the factory. Such trips were not always productive. The atmosphere just wasn't compatible; too much business and not enough play.

It was a known fact that Jim Cabela loved to fish so I thought we should change the location of the next meeting. I adjusted the itinerary to a favorite fishing location, where we all enjoyed fishing, socializing and work. The meeting was such a success, we decided to keep it there in the future. The factories involved later complimented me, saying, "This was the best customer and factory meeting we've ever had." Jim's passion for fishing helped to give me the idea that changed the atmosphere of our meeting forever.

—J.E. "Buster" Coffey
Sales Rep

Goose Interrupted

Cabela's has five goose-hunting pits for the employees to use in the fall, but you have got to put your name on the list to use them well ahead of time. I had reserved one of the pits for a Saturday morning and my brother and his buddy backed out at the last second, so I ended up going alone.

Just as a small flock of geese rose from the roost and began flying in my direction, I noticed two hunters out in the field heading toward me. I figured they were heading for pit #2, which was vacant. I forgot about them and turned my concentration back to the geese.

The geese veered long before they reached the pit, but I could hear the excitement in the voices of the others still on the roost and knew it would not be long before they were in the air. I had spotted a lone goose coming out of the east and was just getting ready to coax it in a bit closer with my call when the lid to the pit slid open. To my astonishment two people began to climb down the ladder. I was speech-less. We had four pits and I was the only hunter in any of them. These two just stroll over to my pit and jump in as if they owned the place. Well, it turned out that they did. When they pulled their hoods off, my mom and dad smiled and said, "Thought you could use some company."

I had initially thought two rude people had ruined my hunt for the day, but, it turned out to be one of the most memorable goose hunts I have ever been on. We watched the geese fly all day, shot a few and missed a few more, but all in all, it was a great day. I got to spend the day with two people I love dearly, doing something I love to do. It was one of those days which remind you what is important and why we need more days like this one.

—Rich Cabela
Liquidation Manager

5₀ | *The Invention of the Telephone*

*T*ODAY, A LARGE PORTION OF ORDERS filled by Cabela's are received over the telephone. Now, instead of going through all the work of taping coins to a piece of cardboard, customers have the option of calling a toll-free number to place their orders.

This faster method of order placement was not introduced at Cabela's until 1978. Before then, a few customers preferred to call instead of spending time filling out an order form and mailing it in. As the number of these consumers grew, Cabela's could see another major change was headed their way.

Dick remembers the implementation of the telemarketing department well:

"I was at the Direct Marketing Association Conference when phone calls from customers was first discussed. It wasn't even called telemarketing then. It consisted of handling a group of consumers who seemed too lazy to fill out the order blank and mail it to you. The phone calls were from individuals who wanted voices on the end of the line in place of sending mail. We considered them a pain in the backside . . . but knew they had to be dealt with. We advertised our Nebraska phone number and then we were forced to hire phone operators to handle this influx of calls."

As the company expanded, the telemarketing department naturally grew with it. In the early years of receiving calls there was not a toll-free number for Cabela's, so the customers using this method had to pay for their calls and, in some instances, had trouble getting through.

All calls were distributed by a switchboard operator, who had to use an old Northwestern Bell switchboard featuring two consoles, one for incoming calls and the other for the extension buttons. There were eighteen incoming lines handling customer orders, customer-service calls, business calls and personal calls. Frequently, the operator had to deal with eighteen lines ringing at once, not to mention a great deal of stress.

By 1981 the telemarketing department had jumped to fifteen employees and was moved to the third floor. Shortly after, management decided to retire the old switchboard and replace it with the company's first automatic call-distribution system.

As telemarketing expanded the problems did not disappear. Most of the time the problems merely changed, or worse, grew right along with the department. Sometimes the telemarketing people wished the telephone had never been invented. It seemed as if every time a problem or glitch was taken care of another would immediately arise. As soon as the employees got used to the old system a new, and "much better" one would come along and they would have to start over. Through the years, most of the kinks have been worked out and the in-bound telemarketing department at Cabela's is one of the best to be found anywhere.

In the early days of the company, Cabela's employees were not always the only people who had trouble with telephones. Mike Wieser, Divisional Merchandise Manager of Hunting and Optics remembers one of these instances:

"When I was working in our old retail store in downtown Sidney, the telephone company sent a repairman to hook up another line next to the cash register. He had drilled a hole through the floor to extend a cable to the basement. Attempting to clean out the hole, he got his finger stuck in it. He sat there next to the cash register for about an hour until another guy from the telephone company came to help him get his finger out. Our customers waiting to check out seemed to find his predicament very amusing."

Later in 1982 Dick was confronted with a telemarketing suggestion he was not sure about:

"It was proposed to place an 800 number in our catalog. Now we were expected to hire someone to answer the call and pay for the call ourselves? I'll have to admit I was not pleased with the concept. And then I found out we could recommend the customer purchase the blue shirt if the green one was out of stock. We could also suggest they purchase some line to go with that new fishing reel. About twenty percent of the customers took advantage of the special offered item of the day and we were selling some overstocked merchandise. All of a sudden this 800-number thing began to make sense."

The toll-free 800 number was initiated in April of 1983. Many more customers began ordering by phone when they no longer had to pay for the calls themselves. The telemarketing department employment rose to sixty full-time employees by 1985, and during the Christmas rush the number had to be boosted up to one hundred.

The growth of the telemarketing department was directly related to the expansion of the company as a whole. The former John Deere building had sustained the company's growth of more than twenty-five percent a year since 1969. However, by the end of 1985 it was apparent that further expansion was necessary.

Dick and Jim knew they needed more space and more employees:

"Twenty-five percent growth per year was more than we had anticipated and it appeared that there was no end in sight to this steady growth. We had quadrupled our business from 1979 to 1984 and we did not have a choice but to expand. We already employed over 400 full-time employees in a town of only 6000. If we were going to be able to sustain our pattern of growth, then our expansion would have to be to another city which could handle our employment needs."

Cabela's found an ideal location in 1986. There was an old Rockwell International plant in the town of Kearney, Nebraska, which had been empty for over a year. Located about 200 miles east of Sidney, Kearney is a college town with a population around 28,000, a number which increases by 7,000 in the fall, when classes resume. Cabela's moved the bulk of telemarketing to Kearney that year.

With a larger employment base, consisting primarily of an enthusiastic college-community workforce from the University of Nebraska-Kearney, Cabela's found the answer to the tedious job of taking phone orders twenty-four hours a day. In addition, the new building already had an established warehouse facility which would enhance the Sidney-based operation.

The new operation employed close to 100 people immediately, and by November of 1986, employment was above 300. The majority were in the telemarketing department, but the opening of a new retail outlet also added to the total number of employees.

The Kearney retail store had the same general theme as the Sidney store, creating a unique shopping experience in an outdoor atmosphere. The wildlife displays in both facilities soon became a tourist attraction as well as a place to shop. There were more than 250 wildlife mounts and live native Nebraska fish in over 4,000 gallons of water in three aquariums in Kearney alone.

Rapid development provided its own silent testimonial to the ever-growing, worldwide renown of the corporation. 1988 saw the addition of more phone lines and the purchase of a computer program to aid in scheduling operators. Thousands of calls poured in daily, leading to the purchase of a sophisticated call-distribution system in August of 1989, an all-digital, automatic call distributor manufactured by Infoswitch. In addition to being on the leading edge of technology with its state-of-the-art equipment, the telemarketing area was also recognized as one of the few places where AT&T had a "point of presence," a central communication point serving a geographic area, on the private property of the user's site.

Dick Cabela has no doubt that the company could never have sustained its substantial growth without keeping up with technological advances:

"I have to admit that much of today's technology has passed me by personally. However, Cabela's has kept up with the rapidly changing technological world. If we had not seen the importance of technological advancement early in the game, we never would have survived. Although sometimes I have been reluctant to spend so much on our mainframe computers, I'll have to concede they were worth every penny and have easily paid for themselves."

Though projections seemed fairly high for the Kearney retail store, they were nearly doubled in the first few years. It seems quite amazing that the growth of the Kearney facility was not at the expense of the Sidney-based operations. For the same period in which Kearney doubled projections, Sidney enjoyed double-digit increases across the board.

While the Kearney facility had opened and enjoyed quick growth, the distribution system in Sidney was becoming more cost-efficient. The summer of 1985 saw the beginning of the UPS Drop Shipment Program. This allowed items to be shipped from UPS centers regionally located closer to the customer, which improved delivery time.

In 1988 the company invested in an in-motion sealing-scanning system. This system was capable of scanning a bar code with the customer's name, address, and customer number. In addition, the system automatically enters the information into the computer system. By 1990, two more of these systems were added. Each system has the capacity to scan thirty-four packages a minute, or approximately 2,000 per hour.

In the ever-changing technological world no business could survive without the flexibility to change with it. My father and uncle realized this but were still sometimes reluctant to spend the amount of money these changes often involved. Even so, they have not let Cabela's fall behind the advances of technology.

Cabela's approach to the catalog operation, as a whole, is somewhat unique in the direct-mail industry. In the beginning years, budget restraints made it necessary for Dad, Mom, Jim and their first employees to do almost everything by themselves. Though budget constraints are not what they used to be, Cabela's still uses that hands-on approach in the catalog operation. Copywriting, photography, typesetting, merchandising, product evaluation, warehousing, and shipping are all completed by on-site employees.

The growth which Cabela's, Incorporated has sustained is astonishing, especially when we consider that it all started as a kitchen-table hobby. I grew up witnessing much of this development and every time I think about it I am amazed and filled with pride.

Bob Archibald Sr., one of the early sales representatives who traveled to Sidney to call on Cabela's, saw first-hand how the values of Jim, Dick and Mary are almost always shared by the rest of the company:

"From the time I started calling on Cabela's, both Jim and Dick have always treated the sales reps with courtesy and respect. There are a lot of places where someone can buy hunting gear, but as far as the sales reps are concerned, Cabela's wrote the bible."

I would like to share a few numbers which are utterly mind-boggling. In 1961, Dick and Mary offered only one product to consumers, a set of hand-tied flies. In 1998, Cabela's offered more than 90,000 products to their patrons. Of those, approximately 45,000 were designed and manufactured specifically for Cabela's.

Sometimes we can faintly hear a hint of astonishment in Dick's voice as he explains some of the products Cabela's now offers:

"Our inventory has grown! The SKU count has escalated from one to over 150,000 active numbers. In 1961, we offered one set of flies. Last year we had a selection of eighteen different assortment packs, plus over 840 individual fishing-fly patterns and sizes. We offer over 150 different styles of boots and shoes . . . hiking, walking, running, standing in water up to your knees or chest, women's, children's and men's. If you are an outdoor enthusiast, we have something to put on your feet or on your dog's feet. Our Alaskan Iditarod Dog Booties were used by the dogs at the rescue effort after the Oklahoma City bombing. There are fly-fishing rods, spinning rods, bait-casting rods, trolling rods, and saltwater rods in dozens of lengths. If you took all the rods offered in our catalogs and placed them end to end, the available variety would stretch 10,219 feet. That's the Chicago Sears Tower—times seven!"

Some other extraordinary numbers tell of the catalog distribution. In 1998, the company printed 60,250,000 catalogs to be mailed to current customers, new customer requests and to be used in the retail stores. On average, Cabela's receives 47,000 new catalog requests weekly, 204,000 monthly and 2,444,000 annually.

Dick explains a few of the changes that Cabela's and the catalog industry have undergone over the years:

"That first mail drop fit in the trunk of my car. Now we mail approximately 60,000,000 catalogs annually. For the 1997 season we mailed twenty-six titles. This expansion of catalogs has been spurred by consumer demand for specific, unique items. We have books offering distinctive products, such as fly-fishing which contain over 260 rods designed exclusively for this sport. The camping catalog has more than

100 pages of merchandise guaranteed to keep you comfortable in the woods. The archery book offers over sixty different bows in a variety of sizes. The 100-plus page shooting catalog displays a wide assortment of equipment for this sport. The marine catalog is filled with electronic equipment and safety gear. Very few titles combine more than one area of interest. The days of mailing huge catalogs offering a large variety of goods are dead and gone. We are living in a time-conscious society. Customers don't have time to wade through page after page of products they don't want. Ten years ago catalogs were a form of entertainment. Now, with rare exceptions, they are simply a quick, easy method of purchasing wares."

My dad fails to mention that those rare exceptions often involve a Cabela's catalog. I have personally witnessed people leafing through Cabela's catalogs just to look at the items offered. Many times I have entered the bathrooms of acquaintances to find that the stack of reading material is topped off with a Cabela's catalog. One time, I was waiting in line at the Department of Motor Vehicles, which everyone knows can sometimes last hours, when I turned around to see a young woman salivating over the pages of an open Cabela's catalog. Most likely she was trying to decide how many items she could afford to purchase for the upcoming hunting season.

The methods of ordering the products offered through the catalogs have changed drastically since Dick, Mary and Jim entered into the mail-order industry. In the beginning years of the company almost all orders came in the mail. Rarely would a customer call to place an order. Eventually, consumers wanted the convenience of placing an order over the phone. Their orders could be processed immediately, allowing faster delivery and it was easier to call in an order to a knowledgeable operator, who could answer questions, than to fill out an order form and send it in. In 1997, 79% or 3.6 million orders were received over the phone with the remaining 21% coming through the mail. Phone orders are no longer seen as a nuisance, but are the backbone of the mail-order industry. With the public's acceptance of the Internet, online sales are quickly gaining ground.

As a result of the change in customer behavior, the telemarketing department has multiplied from three employees to an average of 560, with a peak of 1,500 during the busy season. Telemarketing has also expanded into three separate Nebraska communities, North Platte, Grand Island, and Kearney.

The telemarketing department is not the only area which has seen a substantial development. The entire operation has grown from Mary and Dick at their ten square feet of kitchen table to over 6,000 employees in seven cities, in three states and approximately 2.5 million square feet.

Cabela's has expanded to areas outside of Sidney. With a population of 6,000, Sidney could not sustain the company's booming growth. Cabela's expansion has not been costly to the Sidney area, but quite the contrary. Sidney has, in fact, benefited greatly from the company's outside growth. With almost 1,200 employees in Sidney alone, Cabela's is the largest employer in the area.

The company's growth since 1961, when my father ran

that first simple classified ad, is like that of an excitable puppy maturing into a skilled hunting dog which seems to bag more birds each new day in the field. With that said, where else on earth are there the opportunities for anyone to turn a humble idea into a dream come true . . . Only in America. Dad and Jim are proof of that old cliché. They truly believe that their dream was brought to life by a combination of factors—hard work, perseverance, talented employees and loyal patrons who keep coming back and continue to tell their friends about Cabela's, The World's Foremost Outfitter.

𝟞₀ | *Retail Expansion*

WHEN CABELA'S WAS IN ITS EARLY YEARS, Dick and Jim had no plans whatsoever for retail . . . they were solely in the mail-order business.

Mail-order seemed to be the sensible choice for these two brothers from Chappell, Nebraska. Dad and Jim knew outdoor enthusiasts were a widespread and diverse group of consumers. Although Chappell and the surrounding communities had their fair share of hunters, anglers and campers, the small local market would have been barely enough for a small, unknown retail outfit selling only sporting goods to survive.

Luckily, Dick and Jim have never been nearsighted. If they had not looked at the bigger picture, and to the future, the world may never have come to know The World's Foremost Outfitter.

When the two brothers had to set up tables near the front door of the Chappell locations to block those early retail customers from walking through the inventory, they started to realize that retail had some potential.

That potential did not begin to take form, however, until the move to Sidney. In the beginning, retail took up very little space in the newly acquired Sidney facility. The small area was more than enough to service the local community for a few years. But as inventory grew, and the retail portion of the building acquired more mounts to display, word got out that Cabela's Incorporated now had a retail showroom, and expansion became necessary.

At first, they moved other departments from the first floor to the second and third floors and expanded retail little by little on the main floor. The company was accumulating more discontinued items and returned products. They decided retail should expand to include most of the basement. Discontinued and returned merchandise was sold in the basement at discounted prices and thus the "Bargain Basement" at Cabela's was created.

When the company expanded telemarketing to Kearney, retail expansion soon followed. Although the Sidney retail store enjoyed patrons from all over the country, the Kearney facility brought forth new opportunities. The majority of Nebraska's residents live in the eastern half of the state in cities such as Omaha, Lincoln and Grand Island. Kearney, three hours closer to these larger cities, had a population of its own that was almost five times that of Sidney's.

Although the Kearney retail outlet was much closer to a larger population, it did not mean there was no risk involved. Many outdoorsmen and women tend to live in smaller communities farther away from the larger cities. A large investment of time and money was put into the Kearney facility; failure may not have meant certain doom for the company, but it would have been a significant setback. Dick and Jim are known for taking calculated risks which almost always turn to gold, and the Kearney retail store was no exception. Customers accepted the facility with open arms and before long the numbers had surpassed all expectations.

In 1991, the company built a catalog showroom along Interstate 80 in Sidney, which resulted in the catalog coming to life. With this new retail outlet, Cabela's succeeded in creating an outdoor atmosphere for a unique shopping experience. Such a task required a lot of space. The catalog showroom encompasses 75,000 square feet of building and the entire complex sits on forty-five acres. The showroom ceiling is fifty-two feet above the floor.

The company gives its own brief description of the catalog showroom:

> "Our Sidney retail store rises some fifty-five
> feet above the Nebraska prairie, with over 500
> trophy mounts. The focal point of the trophy
> display is Conservation Mountain, with over

forty individual mounts on rugged terrain that includes high country rock, glacial formations, prairie, and hardwood forest. A gun library becomes an integral part of the hunting department, with collectible, investment, and limited-edition arms available. Finally, the High Plains Cache deli restaurant provides a respite for the traveler, as well as Cabela's customer family. Buffalo, smoked turkey and ham, and several unique menu items reflect the namesake's tradition."

The building is filled with nearly every item in the catalogs, plus a few special ones for retail only. Another reason Cabela's Catalog Showroom has become an important destination for outdoor enthusiasts is its outdoor atmosphere, featuring more than 500 mounted animals, the 8,000-gallon aquariums, and the mountain—forty-eight feet deep, twenty-six feet wide and twenty-seven feet tall, displaying forty game mounts from throughout North America, which Cabela's proudly calls its "Tribute to Sportsmen." Other features include a full-mounted African elephant and a hippopotamus.

Upon first entering the massive building, customers and tourists alike cannot help but look up in awe at the sheer size of the store. While doing so, their eyes focus on a flock of seventeen Canada Geese with wings set, ready to come in for a landing. As they lower their eyes, they immediately see two trophy bull elk in battle. The same elk scene can be seen outside the building with T.D. Kelsey's bronze sculpture called "Royal Challenge," which is sixteen feet high and thirty-four feet across.

The main walkway is lined on both sides with massive pillars made from Colorado moss rock, each sporting a huge trophy bull elk shoulder mount. The 8,000-gallon freshwater aquarium is divided into four 2,000-gallon sections, each containing designated species of fish, including trout, panfish, gamefish, and predator fish.

The Bargain Basement has evolved into the Bargain Cave, with the creation of Cabela's Catalog Showrooms, but the idea of the Bargain Basement is the same. Some items in the Bargain Cave are slightly damaged returns, or one-of-a-kind, but many are merely overstock from discontinued items no longer sold in the catalogs. The one thing all of these products have in common is that they can be found in the Bargain Cave marked down to low (many times ridiculously low) prices. Many ecstatic customers leave the Bargain Cave sporting huge smiles and explaining to their friends how flabbergasted they were to get the product they had purchased at such a low price.

To get an idea of the entire size of the complex, consider the parking lot between the 70,000-square-foot facility and a three-and-a-half-acre pond. The parking lot provides enough spaces for four hundred fifty cars and trucks. In addition, another section has spaces available for forty semi-trucks, RV's and camper units.

Even though Cabela's attempted to keep the opening of

the store relatively quiet, more than 3,000 customers visited the store during the first day of business. One of the most amazing bits of information about the catalog showroom in the small rural town of 6,000, in the Nebraska Panhandle, is that this unique retail experience has become the number-one tourist attraction in the entire state. In 1998, an estimated 840,000 customers and tourists visited Cabela's Catalog Showroom on the sparsely populated plains.

The Grand Opening, held shortly after the store was up and running, was a much bigger event. Bob Archibald, Sr. remembers that even though Dick was extremely busy and had not worked the sales floor in more than ten years, he found the time for a customer who happened to catch him in the showroom:

"During the Grand Opening of the huge retail store in Sidney, I was on the floor working Walls clothing when a guy came up to me with an ad from the newspaper and asked me where this guy named Cabela was. Boy was he mad. He said the binoculars in the ad didn't match the ones that were for sale and he wanted to see one of the Cabelas. Just as we were discussing this, Dick came walking by and offered to help. The customer accused Dick of misrepresenting his products in the ad. Dick proceeded to help him out and politely showed him there was no mistake. Dick went out of his way to make this guy happy. To no surprise, the guy purchased the binoculars and asked Dick to autograph the newspaper ad."

One day I spent a couple of hours near the entrance of the store watching people's reactions and speaking to a few of the patrons coming in. Nearly all were in awe and gazing in admiration. The most common non-verbal reaction was a slowed step and a dropped jaw as visitors came through the doors and discovered a museum-like atmosphere.

Some of the visitors spoke of the sheer size of the place, and the mountain is always a popular topic. The gun room and the High Plains Cache, a sandwich shop serving buffalo subs and other sandwiches, are also favorite subjects for those not too awestruck to speak.

The catalog showroom in Sidney defies one of the major themes taught in the retail world. Experts say the three most important aspects of running a successful retail store are location, location, and location. Cabela's Catalog Showroom in Sidney proves there are exceptions to that rule. I have spoken to many hunters and anglers from all over the country who plan their annual trips, with a stop in Sidney "required." More than a simple retail store, the showroom has become a vacation destination for many outdoor enthusiasts. Customers have remarked many times that Cabela's is the candy store for the outdoor enthusiast.

This is in direct violation of the rule of location. Sidney lies 180 miles from Denver, the closest metropolitan center. Sidney's remote location cannot be overstated, but this has not deterred customers and tourists from flocking to the small community to visit Cabela's.

Sidney's small municipal airport has become as busy as a beehive with Cabela's fly-in customers diving down in planes, gathering merchandise from the showroom and soaring back into the sky. Cabela's provides an airport shuttle bus and on many days more than sixty planes land in Sidney so the travelers can shop at the catalog showroom.

By nature, I hate to go shopping, but I must admit, I rarely go home to Sidney without making a visit to the store. Shopping at Cabela's is a unique shopping experience. Like most hunters and anglers I lick my chops while I stare at all of the outdoor merchandise, wishing I could have it all.

The outdoor products available are only half of the experience. A person can spend hours just wandering and admiring the wonderful taxidermy, with trophy mounts of animals and fish that hunters and anglers spend their lifetimes pursuing.

I truly believed I would never discover another shopping experience that surpassed or even equaled time spent in Cabela's Catalog Showroom in Sidney. Boy, was I wrong. In my own defense, I never thought another catalog showroom would be built, and even if it were, how could it be better than the one in Sidney? The answer is not to make it better, but bigger, a lot bigger.

When my dad first told me about the plans for the new store, I could hear the excitement in his voice. He said the new store would be twice as big as the Sidney retail store and the traffic which traveled by the Owatonna, Minnesota location was seven times more than the traffic going by Sidney on Interstate 80. Twice the size of the Sidney store sounded awfully big to me, but I was still unprepared for the sheer size of the facility when I stepped across the threshold in April of 1998.

Cabela's Owatonna retail establishment encompasses 150,000 square feet, with the ceiling fifty-five feet above the floor. Owatonna is located about fifty miles south of Minneapolis on Interstate 35. The Land of 10,000 Lakes offers a huge market of outdoor enthusiasts but, like the Sidney store, attracts visitors from all over the world. By July more than one million customers and tourists had already visited. In the first year, Cabela's Owatonna store recorded almost four million visitors. These numbers surpassed all expectations.

For an idea of the sheer size of the facility, when we first visited the store there were twenty-four of us. My wife, Shari, and I split away from the group and explored on our own. A little over an hour had passed before we ran into any of our other twenty-two companions. The time had streaked by and we hadn't even explored one quarter of the building. We had spent close to an hour admiring the massive mountain display alone.

The mountain is ninety-eight feet deep, eighty-eight feet wide and thirty-five feet tall. There are more than one hundred mounts of animals, found throughout North America, on the mountain alone. These mounts are all displayed in real-life situations offering a unique, emotional, and educational experience. With more than seven hundred animals throughout the showroom, the atmosphere is one of the wilderness come to life indoors. The wildlife scenes bring back cherished memories of time spent in the field witnessing similar events.

The showroom boasts two African displays in natural settings featuring African wildlife harvested by Dick and Mary Cabela. My parents are especially proud of those displays and how they capture the wildlife in natural and realistic situations. They both have fallen in love with Africa since the first time they traveled there in the late 1980's. The African dioramas are their way to try to share some of their African experiences with Cabela's loyal patrons.

The aquariums are another frequent stop for visitors as they wander for hours through one of the largest hunting, fishing and outdoor-gear stores in the nation. Collectively, the aquariums hold approximately 54,000 gallons of water. The waters are filled with gamefish found throughout Minnesota waters.

Before you enter the showroom your sight will feast upon a huge sculpture, three times the real-life size, of two majestic white-tailed deer. Created by wildlife artist Dick Idol, "Autumn Legends" measures $26^1/2$ feet tall and weighs eight tons. The two white-tails which inspired the sculpture can be seen on display in an identical pose just as you enter the store. One of the deer's antlers is a record from a deer so cunning and elusive it was never taken by a hunter. The shed antlers were found in a field near North Platte, Nebraska.

The master catalogs often display photographs of the different showrooms and some of the wildlife scenes within. Although pictures cannot do justice to the atmosphere and size of the facility, they offer a taste of what Cabela's customers can see.

Cabela's brief description of the Owatonna store echoes with pride:

> Cabela's world-class retail environment in Owatonna offers a new level of shopping experience. Uniquely designed and decorated, the store is much more than a retail facility. It's a complete outdoor experience—indoors! Magnificent trophy displays re-enact true-to-life animal encounters in natural habitat settings.
>
> But, it is the merchandise that is clearly the focus. Cabela's world-famous selection of the finest, field-tested and performance-proven gear showcases the newest technological breakthroughs alongside the time-proven, traditional favorites of outdoor sportsmen and women worldwide.
>
> Come visit. Educational and awe-inspiring, Cabela's retail store is a sight to behold.
>
> Our real-life trophy displays depict actual outdoor encounters, with natural habitat and unique mounts. Each reveals an educational twist to museum-quality dioramas and displays.

Cabela's retail showrooms are unique in so many ways. A superiority in customer service extends to these retail departments. Many of Cabela's customers arrive via air transportation. How many other retail facilities provide a special shuttle bus to take their consumers to and from the airport? Cabela's has always provided this service free of charge.

Of course, the company did not always have a special shuttle van. When I was teenager I worked as a retail clerk in the downtown Sidney store and many of us were called upon from time to time to drive to the airport and pick up customers who had flown in. I often used my own car, but the company did have an old tan van which could be used if and when it was running. Conveniently, the Owatonna showrooom is located very close to the airport.

The restaurant at the showroom in Owatonna seats 125 and offers elk, bison, ostrich, turkey and other standard fare. From its second-story elevation you can enjoy the sights of the store while having a great meal.

Another feature is a live-bait shop. In the Land of 10,000 Lakes, Cabela's would not be complete without one. The visitors can also try out the F.A.T.S. (Firearms Training System), an interactive firearm and archery-training system to test or hone their shooting skills.

The fine gun library in the Owatonna Showroom is second to none. The firearm enthusiast cannot help but spend hours, and sometimes huge sums of money, in the luxurious atmosphere of the library. The library offers classic, antique, collectible and fine sporting firearms. The selection is phenomenal, offering everything from a Winchester 94 Canadian 30-30 to an original 1860 Henry repeating rifle. In addition, Cabela's offers appraisals through the gun libraries in Sidney and Owatonna.

The grand opening of the Owatonna Showroom was quite a sight. It was held from May 30th to June 7th of 1998, and more than 50,000 visitors were welcomed each weekend. Many celebrities of the outdoor world helped to kick off that opening. They included Jeff King, three-time Iditarod Trail Sled Dog Race Champion; Bud Grant, Pro Football Hall of Fame Coach, who led the Minnesota Vikings to four NFC Championships; Chuck Yeager, the first man to fly faster than the speed of sound; and Tom Osborne, who was the winningest active college football coach in the country at the time of his retirement and who coached the Nebraska Cornhuskers to three national championships. Others included Dick Idol, Craig Boddington, Denny Brauer, Chuck Adams, Myles Keller and Gary Roach. The list of outdoor celebrities goes on and on.

The success of the Owatonna Catalog Showroom has not detracted sales from the two Nebraska facilities in Sidney and Kearney. In fact, both have enjoyed increased sales since the opening of the Owatonna Showroom. In addition, the percentage of retail business steadily climbed during the 1990's. The company went from virtually no retail in 1962 to 8.5 percent of business through retail in 1997. And in 1998 the portion of retail business was just over sixteen percent—a substantial jump from the previous year.

In October 1998, Cabela's opened yet another catalog showroom in Prairie du Chien, Wisconsin, a town of 5,500 on the Mississippi River about halfway between Minneapolis and St. Louis. The 40,000-square-foot showroom is connected with a 700,000-square-foot distribution center. A catalog order department allows customers to choose any item from one of the Cabela's catalogs and have the order filled within minutes, literally. The design and theme of the retail store carry on the tradition of bringing the outdoors inside.

The decision to place a catalog showroom next to the distribution center made great sense. Other good reasons for Cabela's to open the new retail store in this particular location were that Prairie du Chien is a popular destination for outdoor enthusiasts and that there is a reliable and competent work force available in the area. Cabela's had been impressed with the people hired at the distribution center and were certain they would see the same results in the retail showroom.

A thirty-five-foot-high mountain with top-quality trophy mounts is Cabela's tribute to sportsmen and women for their continued efforts in conservation. The mountain displays North American game animals of trophy quality in their natural habitat. The display also includes a waterfall and small pond with live trout, giving the natural setting an even more authentic look.

The Prairie du Chien Catalog Showroom sports many of the same features as the other retail facilities, including the Bargain Cave and an aquarium with live, native Wisconsin game fish. In the first few months the store was open in 1998, October through December, the showroom enjoyed almost 200,000 visitors.

In addition to the catalog showrooms in Sidney, Kearney, Owatonna and Prairie Du Chien, Cabela's opened its fifth retail store in September of 1999. The new 60,000-square-foot retail showroom in East Grand Forks, Minnesota has the same atmosphere as all the showrooms, with hundreds of high-quality trophy mounts, a thirty-five-foot mountain, an 8,000-gallon game-fish aquarium, the Bargain Cave, an in-store coffee bar and an indoor firearm-testing area.

The catalog showrooms are similar in atmosphere but each store has a character all its own, just as each trophy mount has its own stories and unique features. Much like the other showrooms, the mountain in East Grand Forks is one of the exceptional specialties. The thirty-five-foot-high mountain displays North American big game trophies in natural habitats and situations. The mountain also features a waterfall which drops into a small beaver pond that empties into a stream flowing into another pond highlighted with live trout. A bridge over the stream allows customers a great view as they head toward the coffee and soft drink bar to sample fresh sandwiches, salads and other menu items. A huge statue of two battling moose titled "Northern Challenge" by Beverly Paddleford adorns the entrance of the facility, preparing visitors for one of the most imaginative shopping experiences they will ever encounter.

Cabela's, and the East Grand Forks community, hope the addition of the catalog showroom will boost the area's economic restoration and re-growth efforts needed since the damaging floods of 1997.

The heart and soul of Cabela's is the catalog division, but the retail division has quickly become more than just a complement to the catalogs. The retail showrooms have become an integral part of the World's Foremost Outfitter. With the continued success of the existing catalog showrooms, it would be safe to say that more retail expansion is in Cabela's future.

Two new catalog showrooms opened in 2000, one in the spring and one in the fall. Opening these new retail stores is a huge undertaking and two stores in a year is about the maximum number plausible. Unlike discount stores, which are essentially shells filled with merchandise, Cabela's takes great pride in making each showroom like an outdoor arena where customers can buy their hunting, fishing and outdoor gear.

Both stores are similar in style and outdoor atmosphere to the other catalog showrooms. One of the most notable differences of the two will be size. The showroom in Mitchell, South Dakota is 85,000 square feet, comparable in size to the Sidney store. In contrast, the showroom in Dundee, Michigan is Cabela's largest retail store to date. At over 200,000 square feet, the Dundee store rises high above the Michigan landscape, beckoning outdoor enthusiasts with its unmistakable giant green roof.

The retail store in Mitchell, South Dakota opened in April of 2000. Considering that South Dakota is world-famous for its pheasant hunting and Mitchell is surrounded by prime hunting country, the city seems to be a perfect fit for a Cabela's Catalog Showroom. The store is expected to attract around 1.5 million visitors every year from all over, as many hunters and anglers travel to South Dakota for its many opportunities for outdoor activity.

The store in Mitchell employs more than 200 people, the majority being from the area. Mitchell has always been a hunting and fishing community and was once home to another outdoor gear company. In fact, Dennis Highby, who has been with Cabela's for twenty-five years and is now vice president of merchandising, fulfillment and retail operations, once worked for Herter's whose headquarters were at one time found in Mitchell.

The addition of Dennis into the Cabela corporate family was mutually beneficial. As an executive of another sporting goods company he brought a profitable expertise to one of the fastest growing outdoor outfitting companies.

Dick Cabela has always given tons of praise to Dennis for all he has done for the corporation:

"Dennis came to Cabela's from Herter's and was a great addition to our company. His commendable work ethic and outstanding business savvy have been key in guiding the World's Foremost Outfitter to the next level and beyond. The commitment and leadership he has brought will ensure we stay on course for the future."

Some of the features in the Mitchell retail store include a 10,000 gallon aquarium with interactive touch-screen kiosks informing visitors about the fish and their native habitats, the famous Cabela's Bargain Cave, a giant bronze sculpture titled "Corn Stalking," by Beverly Paddleford, displaying a fox flushing pheasants; wood furnishings recovered from forests devastated by fire; wildlife dioramas; a Gun Library; a shuttle service and, of course, a mountain replica featuring North American wildlife.

In the fall of 2000 Cabela's opened its largest retail store yet in Dundee, Michigan. With more than 200,000 square feet, the new showroom in Dundee is, amazingly, bigger than the Owatonna store by at least 50,000 square feet. The retail facility is part of a 150-acre complex which will eventually host hotels, restaurants and service stations.

Experts at Cabela's believe the new showroom will become the state's top tourist attraction. Much of the predictions are based on the success of the Owatonna Showroom, which hosted over four million visitors in its first year. It is predicted that the retail store will draw more than six million visitors annually.

Cabela's Catalog Showrooms have come to be known as much more than retail stores, and are often destinations for family vacations. The museum-like wildlife displays alone are worth the visit, even if no purchase is planned.

Located about thirty miles southwest of Detroit along Interstate 23, the showroom is clearly visible to a high number of travelers. The roadway is used by many outdoor enthusiasts on their way to or from some of the country's beautiful outdoor areas. Michigan and the surrounding states have long-standing outdoor recreation traditions, with outstanding hunting, fishing and camping opportunities in nearby Canada as well.

More than 600 people are needed to run the new showroom, with the majority of the employees, once again, coming from the areas surrounding the facility. Cabela's eagerly embraces the opportunity to establish a physical presence in the state of Michigan where many of Cabela's loyal customers live. The city of Dundee showed great interest and was enthusiastic about a partnership with Cabela's and their community.

The new store is like the other showrooms, featuring an enormous mountain with realistic wildlife displays; the Bargain Cave; a service bay where vehicle accessories can be installed on a customer's boat or automobile; a service department for all outdoor gear; an auditorium and educational center available for seminars, conventions and school groups; a walk-through aquarium with a capacity of over 60,000 gallons; a huge bronze sculpture, by Mike Hamby, depicting two bears fighting over a moose carcass; a Gun Library; interactive firearms and archery laser training systems; a shooting gallery for children where they can learn shooting skills in a safe environment; a live-bait shop; dog kennels; a horse corral; and a parking lot large enough for 1,500 automobiles, 100 semi-trucks, 100 vehicles towing boats or trailers and thirty buses. A few of the Dundee store's unique wildlife displays include an authentic African diorama; A monster Alaskan bull moose wading in a shallow pond, complete with live trout; bubbling brooks and strategically placed beaver ponds hosting live brown, brook and rainbow trout; and a diorama featuring game animals from the South Pacific in their native settings.

Retail stores were not in the initial plans, as running a

catalog company was more than Dick and Jim could handle at first. Even after they decided a retail store could be profitable, they never dreamt how profitable it could be or that the few mounts they placed around the first retail store in downtown Sidney would be the beginning of a chain of museum-quality catalog showrooms. But they never stopped believing it could be bigger and better and they always worked hard to insure that it was.

Mark Wieser was one of the first employees to run the retail department and remembers the store when it was only one room just inside the entryway of the office building:

"I began my association with Cabela's in the early 1970's. During this time, I watched the company grow and did what I could to help it along. I thoroughly enjoyed working in the retail store and remember the $100 a day we were making was pretty slow, but Dick and Jim could visualize the potential and after numerous remodeling jobs to the retail store, business began to increase. The retail department eventually became a substantial part of the company and today the growth is really something to see."

Nobody knows for sure what the future holds for the catalog showrooms, not even Dick and Jim. If the current retail stores continue to show the success and promise they have, then more Cabela's Catalog Showrooms will surely be considered. Who knows, maybe one will open in your hometown some day.

7. The Sidewalk Sale

ONE OF THE MOST EXCITING DAYS for Cabela's retail customers and the catalog showrooms is the company's annual sidewalk sale. Like everything else in the Cabela's story, this annual sale that draws thousands, started with humble beginnings.

Cabela's Sidewalk Sale began in Sidney. The community businesses had been holding annual sidewalk sales before the two Cabela brothers moved their small operation to the town. The sale is held every July and the whole community looks forward to one weekend of bargain shopping. Local businesses take certain items outside their stores, putting them on tables and racks on the sidewalk. They discount the items for sale not only to move more merchandise but also as a form of appreciation to their customers.

Dick and Jim quickly decided to participate in this annual sale. Dick gives us one of the original reasons they looked forward to it:

"The town was having this sidewalk sale and we thought it would be a great opportunity to get rid of some of our back-stock, which included discontinued items and returns. These products were just taking up space and we needed to get rid of them, so we marked the prices way down. If we had known then how big the sale would eventually become, we may have even advertised it."

The first sidewalk sales saw a few local shoppers find some great deals. Each year they found more of them and then they must have told their families and friends, because the crowd at the Cabela's Sidewalk Sale grew yearly without even a hint of advertising.

Before long, word had spread across many state lines that anyone who loved the outdoors could find stunning bargains for their gear on the last Saturday of every July, in Sidney, Nebraska. Every year, consumers who came to this small community passed the word to others that Sidney was a great place to be at the end of July. People came from all over the country looking for the deal of the century. They succeeded and continued to return, many making an annual trip of it. It didn't take long for the number of visitors to Cabela's Sidewalk Sale to reach the thousands. A hike through the parking lot during one of these sales reveals license plates from New York,

Texas, and even Alaska, just to name a few.

By the time the two brothers decided to build their massive catalog showroom next to Interstate 80, the downtown parking lot was pushed past the limits by the influx of people searching for a steal on a new rod, or a pair of boots. The sale had become more of an event than a simple sidewalk sale. Consumers began to come early to wait in line, and eventually started to camp outside the parking lot so they could be the first in line and get the best bargains. A few crowd-control methods were soon needed. The entire area had to be roped off to give some organization to the way the lines formed and to signal the opening of the event, a blast from a shotgun was employed.

I remember one morning before the annual sale began, I was up at the crack of dawn, hoping to catch a few fish at a nearby pond before the sale got into full swing. I thought I would run by the retail store, still located downtown, to see how many customers had shown up early. I was about two blocks from the building when I saw a man standing on top of a motor home peering through a pair of binoculars.

I stopped to ask him what he was looking at. He told me that his wife was saving their place in line at Cabela's while he was scoping out which bargains they would head for first. I wished him luck and continued toward the store.

The line of people waiting was longer than I had expected. There were more than 800 men, women and children waiting for the start of the sale with only a handful from the Sidney area. The looks on the hundreds of faces were of anticipation and excitement—emotions not usually associated with long lines. I decided to find a good spot to sit and watch for a little while.

The crowd rushed forward when the gun sounded and the gates were opened. People literally sprinted to the items they apparently had their eyes on prior to the sale. One of the first in line was a thin, wiry man who was shaking in anticipation of the shotgun blast. When he charged through the gates he ran right by a pile of tents and camping gear and without missing a step, grabbed an assortment of shirts, jackets and sweaters off a rack. He did not sort through anything, he just took all that he could. With the clothing draped over his shoulder, he sprinted to another rack full of chest waders, grabbed as many as he could carry and ran to one of the cashiers to check out. He was in and out of the sale in less than ten minutes with a few hundred dollars' worth of discounted merchandise.

In 1997, the sidewalk sale drew more than 15,000 customers—almost triple the size of Sidney—not bad for an event the brothers never considered advertising before it became such a spectacle. For the town of Sidney, with a population around 6,000, this sale brings a single weekend of economic boom; hotels are filled to capacity, gas stations are pumping tons of fuel and the state patrol has to bring in extra officers to handle the traffic.

Many of the same patrons return each year and have naturally made friends with other consumers. Some families even plan their summer vacations so they can meet two or three days early in the parking lot of Cabela's.

A few years ago, the first person to show up came two weeks early. As tradition holds, the first person in line gets a head start. Therefore, that position is prized each year. In addition, the initial hundred or so get a few extra minutes before the remaining two or three thousand get to enter. This is one of the reasons so many customers come well in advance of the sale.

By the Thursday before the Saturday sale, the parking lot is filled with hundreds of customers saving their places in line. Any night from Wednesday on, you can drive to the parking lot and witness hundreds of people gathered in groups around tents, cooking on grills and enjoying refreshments from over-sized coolers. There are always remarkable stories flying around throughout the night, of exciting hunts or huge fish caught—some of them might even be true. Many of the die-hard customers stay up all night Friday sharing their unique and personal experiences with their old and new friends.

The camaraderie of all these outdoorsmen and women before the sale begins is a testament to the tight bond outdoors enthusiasts share. However, once the sale begins, the competition becomes intense. When that gun goes off, signaling the start of the event, it's everyone for themselves. Groups of two or three often leave one person in charge of guarding the pile of merchandise the others acquire. And they are expected to guard it with their lives. Most customers leave with a smile, boasting to their friends about the unbelievable discounted boots or drastically-marked-down tent they had just purchased.

Mary remembers one customer and friend who found a deal at the sidewalk sale which wasn't quite what he expected: "This particular friend of ours had spotted an extra-large vest at a great price and just had to have it. He was so excited with his bargain he rushed home to show his wife. When he tried to put it on and model it for her he struggled unsuccessfully to get it over his arms. Annoyed, he looked at the tag and was immediately embarrassed to discover the extra-large vest he had just purchased was specifically designed for a dog!"

The event has grown so large that Cabela's has added other attractions to go with their sometimes ridiculously discounted sale items. Some of the past events have included autograph sessions and seminars by Iditarod champion Jeff King; the F.A.T.S. (Firearm Training Systems) interactive shooting system, giving customers a chance to use their hunting and shooting skills on a simulated course; game- and bird-calling seminars; and trick shooting demonstrations by marksmen such as John Satterwhite, former national and international skeet shooting champion.

All of the Sidney businesses participate in the annual Customer Appreciation Day as a way of saying thank you to all those customers who supported the area businesses. However, the Cabela's sale brings anywhere from 10,000 to 15,000 people to the community from more than twenty states, on the last Saturday of each July. One article in the Sidney *Telegraph* stated "Cabela's Sidewalk Sale is like a national holiday for outdoorsmen."

Its growth is nothing short of incredible, especially considering that Cabela's didn't advertise the sale at first, and even now its advertising is minimal. Ninety-five percent of the thousands of people who participate in the annual sale heard about it from the least expensive and most effective form of advertising a business can hope for—word of mouth.

The booming development of the annual sidewalk sale in Sidney closely resembles the steady growth of Cabela's itself. Having started with only a couple of small tables cluttered with products either discontinued or returned, Dick and Jim were hoping they could get rid of some merchandise which was costing them money and taking up valuable space. It is truly amazing how the word spread to attract customers from all over the United States to a small town in the panhandle of Nebraska surrounded by miles of wide open plains. This annual event has been compared to the huge caribou migration but with people coming from all over, congregating in one place with the same goal in mind.

8 | *All in the Family*

DICK CABELA ALWAYS KNEW WHAT INDUSTRY he would end up in:

"My father was a merchant and my grandfather was a merchant. In my eyes there wasn't much of a choice. Selling goods is what my family has always done. It was what I grew up with, what I knew. If it would not have been the flies and eventually outdoor gear, I'm certain it would have been something else. Who knows, I may have kept selling furniture if I had not stumbled across those flies."

Dick and Jim do not remember their family doing anything else, so running their own business seemed quite natural to them. The truth of the matter is the entrepreneurial instincts of James Cabela were passed on to A.C.

whose children and grandchildren have become entrepreneurs themselves. So many of the Cabelas have gone into business for themselves as to prompt some to say entrepreneurism is in their blood.

James Cabela could be considered the primer of the bullet which shot the entrepreneurial spark through generations of the Cabela family. He wanted a better life for his family, and Brainard, Nebraska offered many opportunities, especially in farming and ranching. James tried his hand at farming for about ten years and found some success in it. During his years as a farmer he discovered he had a keen business sense and determined his talents would serve him even better as a merchant so he went to work in town. He saved money until he had enough to go into business for himself, in 1897. Within a few years he was doing so well that he put up a building in downtown Brainard, where he would run a hardware store selling everything from groceries to dry goods such as furnishings and clothing.

He made a name for himself as a proprietor who was honest and upstanding in all his dealings. James was about as prosperous as anyone could be in a tiny town on the plains in the early 1900's. He raised a family and passed on his values, and of course his business sense, to his children.

Two of James Cabela's sons, A.C. and Louis, grew up in Brainard and worked for their father, learning as much as they could about the business. As many young men do, they decided to leave home and find their own place in the world. They left together and traveled to Chappell, Nebraska, where

Dick and Jim in the Sidney showroom, where the catalog comes to life.

Customers rush through the gates at the start of the annual sidewalk sale.

Dick Idol's "Autumn Legends" highlights the catalog showroom in Owatonna, Minnesota.

Dennis Highby with Mary and Dick at the construction of the Owatonna showroom.

Mary, Dick, daughter Cari and daughter-in-law Cathy with Chuck Yeager at Safari Club International Convention.

Above: Africa comes to life in the Owatonna showroom.

Left: Lions attack Zebras in authentic museum quality dioramas.

Right: A look inside one of the distribution centers.

Below: Corporate Headquarters in Sidney.

An aerial view of the distribution center and the showroom in Prairie du Chien, Wisconsin.

Mary, Dick and guide Guy Ventor taking a break from safari in Zimbabwe.

Beverly Paddleford's "Northern Challenge" outside the showroom in East Grand Forks, Minnesota.

Right: "Conservation Mountain" in Sidney showroom. Every showroom has a mountain and each comes with its unique qualities.

Below: An aerial look at the corporate headquarters, catalog showroom and campsite in Sidney.

The Mitchell, South Dakota showroom is highlighted by Beverly Paddleford's "Corn Stalkin'."

Looking through the entrance of the Owatonna showroom is jaw-dropping.

Mike Hamby's "Fierce Encounter" in front of the Dundee, Michigan showroom.

Right: Replicas of some of the world's most famous deer can be found inside the Dundee showroom.

Below: Mary and Dick personally hand out bonus checks and sometimes while they are traveling to the company's locations scattered throughout the Midwest it's hard to tell if they should be at a formal gala or sitting on a tree-stand in the woods.

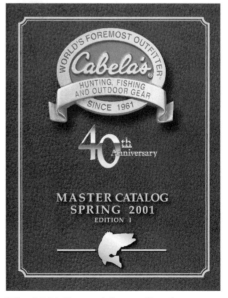

The 2001 Spring Master Catalog.

they purchased a furniture and hardware store from the Chappell Lumber and Hardware Company.

A bit of bad luck surprised the brothers on Halloween in 1935 when the building they had purchased just three years earlier burned down. Determined to persevere, they put the setback behind them and went on. They rented for a couple of years until they could raise the capital to buy another building, which they did in 1937.

The brothers ran the business together until 1942 when Louis moved to Denver and sold his share to A.C. A.C. ran the business with his wife, Marian, and continued to expand until he retired. Under his guidance the company grew from one building that burned down to eight buildings. He had learned well from his father and was highly successful in the business world.

A.C. and Marian raised six children, and their father's and grandfather's business savvy did not slip past them. Their children, Dick, Jim, Diann, Jerry, Jane, and Tom, have all become highly successful in their endeavors and in fact, five of them have gone on to have prosperous businesses of their own.

When A.C. retired, his son Jerry took over the furniture store in Chappell and has continued to offer an honest deal and superb customer service in the tradition of his father and grandfather. Cabela's Furniture in Chappell has grown and expanded under Jerry, just as it did under A.C. The store flourished when A.C. oversaw the operations, and as long as Jerry watches over the company we can feel confident Cabela's Furniture will thrive well into the future.

Dick and Jim's younger sister, Jane, has also heard the entrepreneurial call. She and her husband, Jon Schmid, live in North Platte, Nebraska, where they owned and operated J. Schmid's, a men's clothing store at the North Platte Mall until they closed it in 1999. J. Schmid's became a popular shopping destination for men of all ages in North Platte and the surrounding areas, making it one of the many profitable businesses in the community.

Tom Cabela, the youngest son of Marian and A.C., has done quite well for himself in Lincoln, Nebraska. After college Tom saw an opportunity in the real-estate industry and before long found himself in the property-management business. He has continued to expand and has become respected in his field.

All of Marian and A.C.'s children have put hard work into their businesses and, more important, their lives. Dick, Jim, and their siblings have all, without a doubt, been successful.

The argument can be made that the business sense of my father, aunts and uncles is a direct result of genes passed on from my great grandfather, James, or even from his parents and grandparents, but I believe there is more to it than that.

James Cabela gave A.C. more than just his genes. He taught him that prosperity was possible with hard work and determination, but true success required honesty and integrity as well. James believed an honorable man with no money had more wealth than an ignoble man with unlimited means. He taught A.C. with his words, but more importantly, he taught him with his actions and showed him that how success is achieved is more important than the success itself.

A.C. believed that if he always dealt with people right-eously at Cabela's Furniture Store they would know and they would reward him by returning to do business with him and would, in turn, tell their acquaintances he was an honest dealer. He knew dishonest merchants were rarely in business for long.

Like his father, A.C. taught his children by example and they apparently paid attention. They have all tried to lead their lives with honesty and integrity and have tried to teach their children to do the same, mostly by giving them an example to follow.

On the back of my father's business card is a poem which accentuates the lessons he learned from his father and grand-father long before he went into business for himself. He would show the back of his card to us when he believed we were old enough to truly understand its meaning. The poem speaks for itself:

The Guy in the Glass

BY DALE WIMBROW

When you get what you want in your struggle for pelf,
And the world makes you King for a day,
Then go to the mirror and look at yourself,
And see what that guy has to say.

For it isn't your Father, or Mother, or Wife,
Who judgement upon you must pass.

The feller whose verdict counts most in your life
Is the guy staring back from the glass.

He's the feller to please, never mind all the rest,
For he's with you clear up to the end,
And you've passed your most dangerous, difficult test
If the guy in the glass is your friend.

You may be like Jack Horner and "chisel" a plum,
And think you're a wonderful guy,
But the man in the glass says you're only a bum
If you can't look him straight in the eye.

You can fool the whole world down the pathway of years,
And get pats on the back as you pass,
But your final reward will be heartaches and tears
If you've cheated the guy in the glass.

—Dale Wimbrow 1895–1954

This little poem gains meaning as the years shoot by. When Dad first showed it to me I was a young teenager and thought very little of it, as teenagers tend to do when their parents try to pass on some of the wisdom they have gained through years of experience. Today, I look at the poem and understand why my father had us read it. I can only hope that when I look into the eyes of the guy in the glass I will see half the guy my father sees staring back.

My father and Jim have always been men of few words.

They prefer to let their actions speak for them and most of the lessons my siblings and I have learned from these two have been from examples they have set, not words they have spoken. When Dick has something to say, people are usually all ears. The same can be said for Jim, although his words are, most often, far fewer.

Fred Neal, Cabela's Merchandise Manager of Fishing and Marine, has often seen how much a few words from Jim can say:

"Jim Cabela has a sign on his desk that reads 'Be Brief, Be Blunt, Be Gone' and that pretty well sums up his approach to business. He also has the ability to speak volumes with just a word or two, which can, in most cases, switch the table in Cabela's favor.

"During the late '80's a very large, very well-known manu-facturer of guns, boots, safes and archery equipment and Cabela's were on the verge of a minor falling out. The manufacturer's solution to the problem was to bring a battery of upper-manage-ment types, including the president of the company, to Sidney to intimidate, threaten and browbeat Cabela's into submission. After what seemed like hours of reports, speeches and fist pound-ing, it was finally our turn for rebuttal.

"Jim looked directly at the president with no expression and asked 'Is that it?' Closing his notebook, Jim got up from the table and left without saying another word. Needless to say, those corporate suits had never had a response like that before and were completely dumbfounded. But they left with no doubt where Jim Cabela and the company stood on the matter."

Jim's quiet demeanor is one that demands respect without ever asking for it. He always takes everything in around him and when he has something he wants to say it is apparent he has been paying very close attention.

Jim Townsend remembers the first time he had to make a sales pitch to Jim Cabela:

"The first time I met Jim Cabela was in the fall of 1976 during my first trip to Cabela's as a manufacturer's representative. I will never forget that first appointment.

"Jim came out to the waiting area himself and ushered me back to his office through a maze of halls and offices. I recall his office had very tall ceilings—at least 12 feet—and there were large-paned windows on the front. Jim offered me a chair and took his place behind a substantial oak desk. It struck me that the furnishings and dimensions of the room seemed in contrast to his physical stature.

"He politely asked me what I had to present. As I presented my products, he listened intently without asking any questions. When I finished, he leaned over to open the lower right-hand drawer of his desk and pulled out a piece of paper, which he studied for a few moments. Without any question or comments, he excused himself and left the room for several minutes.

"In his absence, I questioned whether my presentation had been strong enough, and with new-salesman anticipation, I wondered if I should have done anything differently. I sat as patiently as I could, somehow feeling like I was waiting for a verdict.

"My anxiety was ill-founded, for when Jim returned, he handed me a purchase order for over $10,000 and thanked me for coming out to Sidney. I felt it was I who owed thanks, as that order was the largest I had ever received as a rep up to that time.

"As I have grown to know Jim over the years, I think of how my first impression of him told just part of the story. It is true that he is a man of few words, but those words can speak volumes."

The Cabela family has seen entrepreneurs from generation to generation, and if that tradition ended with my father's generation the account would be exceptional. My generation also has a few budding capitalists who have assumed the risk of their own ventures.

Each of Dick's children was taught early the value of hard work. When we were old enough our parents would take us aside and tell us they thought it was time we found a job. We could work at Cabela's if we wanted or we could find a different job if we did not like the terms of working at "the store," as we referred to our parents' and uncle's company at the time.

We could have a job at the store, but we would have to start at the bottom and there would be no special treatment. (Boy, did they mean it!) In fact, some of my siblings still believe that it was harder for them just because their last name was Cabela. It was easy to forget we were given a choice and more than that, an opportunity to feel the rewards from our own work.

Most of us chose to work at Cabela's when we were given

the opportunity and some have stuck it out and are still with the company. We did not all start out doing the same tasks but we all started out right near the bottom with responsibilities ranging from pulling weeds to being an all-around gopher.

Having your teenage boys around the office means they will not be getting into mischief someplace else. Unfortunately, if they are not getting into mischief elsewhere, you can bet you had better keep an eye on them, especially if there are two of them.

Chuck Cabela remembers one time when he and Rich had the whole company angry at them:

"One time Rich and I were alone on the loading dock sweeping the floor. When I saw the circuit breaker nearby, I bet Rich I could turn off the lights without using the light switch. When I pulled the breaker the lights definitely went out. We finished our work and sat down for a break and a laugh. The next thing we knew we were soaked with water.

"Our dad was standing behind us with an empty pitcher and an angry look on his face. We had no idea why he was so angry but soon discovered the circuit breaker was connected to the entire building. When I pulled the switch, not only did the lights go out but the entire building lost power, including every computer."

Eventually, the company got up and running again and all was forgiven. If nothing else, Chuck learned not to pull switches if he wasn't absolutely certain what they were connected to and Dad learned not to leave his kids without supervision if at all possible. Unfortunately, it is impossible to supervise your children all the time, especially when you have nine of them and a company to run. Consequently, they sometimes get themselves into trouble and without thinking about it shut down your business operations!

We weren't always angels, but the time we spent working at the store taught us many important lessons. One significant lesson some of us learned was that being the son or daughter of the boss did not make you special, and that there were many advantages to starting at the bottom of the totem pole. The tasks we had to perform were often the very tasks our parents and our uncle had to carry out at some point. In a small way we were able to see where they came from and why they have always given most of the credit to their hard-working employees.

A few of the nine children Mary and Dick did their best to raise have continued in the entrepreneurial tradition of the Cabela family. They have chosen nine different paths in life, but they have all taken with them the lessons learned working for their parents' company.

Two of my brothers, who have gone into business for themselves, display striking similarities to Dick and Jim. Dan and Joe Cabela own and operate Music Lab, a rehearsal center and recording studio in Austin, Texas. Like Cabela's, Music Lab had very humble beginnings. Dan had found out that making a living as a musician was extremely hard and saw firsthand that there was a need for a rehearsal center in Austin, where the music scene is booming. He leased a building and began to rent out rooms. Joe moved to Austin a few years later and joined the company.

As with Dick and Jim, the talents of the two brothers complemented each other and both men concede that Music Lab would not be what it is today, with its three buildings and ever-growing clientele, if it were not for the other. They have been honest with their customers from the beginning and have offered a fair deal—business practices learned from the generations of Cabela entrepreneurs who came before them.

Far too often when family members try to work together many problems arise, and if those problems cost you a brother or a sister, then, no matter how much money you make, you have failed miserably. Fortunately, Dan and Joe were given an excellent example to follow by their father and uncle.

Dick and Jim's ability to work so closely together maintaining their relationship has sometimes amazed others, especially those with brothers of their own, like J.B. Jorgenson:

"My first recollection of Jim Cabela is meeting with him in a Quonset hut in Chappell, Neb., around thirty years ago. Even though I had some experience with direct mail advertising and the catalog business, I honestly had no expectations for a great future for this account. Jim was pleasantly modest, more polite than many buyers, receptive to my product lines and even ordered some merchandise. I just didn't envision an industry giant rising amidst the grain fields of Nebraska.

"During this visit, Jim phoned his brother to come join us. Dick came over from his dad's furniture store where he was working. He seemed a little more worldly than Jim, maybe because he was a little older. What a great pair! Never in our years of association did I ever hear them express words of disagreement or dissension about anything. Having three brothers myself, I know this shows amazing respect, cooperation and restraint when two brothers work so closely together as partners.

"It didn't take long for me to come to respect and admire the Cabelas for their honesty, genuine sincerity and business acumen. These qualities became evident to their customers, created close relationships with their suppliers and set a standard for their staff and employees to follow."

Another of Dick and Mary's children who has gone into business for himself is Rich Cabela. He continues to work for the company as liquidation manager at Cabela's but also owns and operates Plainman Records with two partners. The record and production company is an after-hours venture for Rich and his partners, just as selling fishing equipment was for Dick in the beginning.

Rich says some of the entrepreneurial drive has to be in the Cabela blood and would bet money that three or four generations from now, James Cabela's descendants will be taking advantage of the opportunities the world has to offer.

Every endeavor cannot be successful, but one can learn a great deal from those that do fail, as Dick and Jim did from their housewares blunder. They found out that, among other things, perseverance is a quality every entrepreneur should learn. They also discovered that if they had not been willing to try something different they may never have understood fully that their true niche was outdoor equipment and not housewares.

Many children follow in their parents' footsteps and sometimes the trails are covered with footprints leading in the same direction for many generations. One noble profession which comes to mind is farming, of which many families can trace their heritage hundreds and even thousands of years back. It seems fitting that James Cabela, who started the trail of entrepreneurs who followed him, was once a farmer, an occupation which traditionally sees many generations understanding the hardships and honor of their ancestors.

Not every Cabela has attempted to start their own business, but enough of them have to make one wonder if there may be something different flowing through their veins which pulls them to the challenge. Most would tell you themselves that all it takes is a little courage to try, and a bit of luck along with a lot of hard work, perseverance and sacrifice to succeed.

My parents and my uncle Jim would remind us that we need to keep our integrity and always be honest. They would also tell us to be careful that in all our successes we do not forget those things which truly matter like faith, family and friends. All the riches in the world can never take the place of the love and joy these things bring into our lives.

9. | *The Customers*

THE TYPICAL CABELA'S CUSTOMER is hard to describe because there is no single type of Cabela's customer. The people who love to shop from and at Cabela's are a diverse group. Men and women of every race from all over the world and from every economic background choose Cabela's for their outdoor gear. The one mutual characteristic that keeps them turning the pages of Cabela's catalogs is their love for the outdoors and wild places.

Traditionally, men have made up a large percentage of Cabela's customers, but traditions are sometimes better left in the past. More and more women have taken to the woods, and in turn need a place to purchase their equipment. And although tradition says Cabela's customers are mostly men, there have always been exceptions. In fact, Cabela's very first customer was a woman. Tradition also tells us that things change and what was once the exception is now the norm. A trip to one of Cabela's retail showrooms proves that there are just as many women shopping in the outdoor atmosphere as there are men, all of them wide-eyed with big grins—mostly because they are passionate about their outdoor equipment, but partly because shopping at one of the showrooms is an adventure in itself, with all the wildlife displays surrounding the merchandise.

Another trait which many Cabela's customers display is consumer loyalty, which has almost become a thing of the past. In today's age of the discount store, few companies manage to keep their customers coming back again and again. Cabela's has had the good fortune to be one of these lucky companies.

Dad tries to explain why he thinks Cabela's customers have been so loyal over the years:

"I don't think there is any one reason why our customers continue to remain loyal to Cabela's. I believe it is a combination of many things that brings the consumers back and prompts them to refer their friends to us. Right up at the top of the list would have to be the products themselves. Our buyers and salespeople all use our products for their outdoor excursions and are very knowledgeable when it comes to answering questions. Exceptional customer service and the 100% satisfaction guarantee are also very important. I think more than anything, the people we hire keep the consumers coming back. Our typical employee is just as passionate about their outdoor gear as most of our customers and those common interests give our customers a personal connection to Cabela's. At Cabela's we sell fun and have fun doing it!"

Most customers order their merchandise from the catalogs, but a large percentage of them will travel long distances to obscure places just to visit and shop at the retail showrooms. Celebrities, politicians, and even royalty from all over the world can occasionally be seen strolling through the outdoor environment of Cabela's, loading up on merchandise, staring and taking pictures of the museum-quality wildlife displays.

Many organizations can claim customers of such social standing but sometimes have the reputation for being too snobbish. This is far from the case at Cabela's, considering that their consumers are just people who love to get outdoors. Cabela's merely sells outdoor products at a fair price that people from all social backgrounds use for their outdoor experiences. Every individual customer is important regardless of social or economic background. The customer is always number one.

Cabela's has its fair share of stories about customers who will do anything to get to one of the showrooms. Many of these events have taken place during the sidewalk sales, but every day there is a new story about how excited a customer was to finally make it to a Cabela's retail store.

One story which comes to mind is when a couple's vehicle caught fire on their way to visit the catalog showroom in Sidney. They only had a few miles left when they had to jump out of their vehicle, which had burst into flames. Their car was destroyed, but when the paramedics arrived on the scene the couple refused to ride in the ambulance. When Cabela's was informed of the situation they sent an employee to pick them up and bring them to the store. That particular couple literally went through fire to make it to Cabela's.

About two miles from Cabela's Catalog Showroom in Sidney is a small airport that has seen an eruption in air traffic. An average of ten small airplanes land at the airport each day carrying people looking forward to doing a bit of shopping at Cabela's. Usually they radio the airport and ask that someone be there when they land. Driving the Cabela's van back and forth to the airport has become a full-time job.

There was one instance when an unknown pilot must have thought the two-mile drive to the airport was too far. Instead of landing at the airport, he landed a single-engine plane in a small field near Cabela's in Sidney. As if it were normal, the pilot then taxied up to the parking lot, left the plane and walked into the store to shop for outdoor gear.

Although the story is amusing now, the local authorities, as well as Cabela's, did not and do not condone dangerous flying. Legal action will certainly be taken if a similar incident ever happens again. The main concern here is safety for other customers and employees. Besides, Cabela's is always more than willing to make a special trip to the nearby airport to pick up pilots and passengers. The ride is less than five minutes and landing on a runway is much smoother than the bumpy fields by Cabela's.

Cabela's customers feel very strongly about their gear and about the company that sells it to them. They come to shop; they come to view the high-quality mounts; they come for conferences; but one couple came for something far more important and personal.

They went to the retail store in Kearney to have their wedding. To those who are not passionate Cabela's customers, this may seem quite strange. Even the most emotional consumers probably do not want to have their wedding in a Cabela's retail showroom, but can understand why others might, the way one angler understands how another angler will spend all day fishing without as much as a nibble and yet go back the next day to try again.

Cabela's receives tons of mail every day from customers complaining or praising. At times the letters are so good (or bad) that they get passed around until half the company knows about them, kind of like an e-mail joke that is so funny everyone sends it to all the names on their lists.

One of the unique gift items Cabela's offers is a jack-rabbit with small deer antlers. One consumer purchased one of these jackalopes and sent it to a family member in England. The gift was detained by customs and soon sent to the Museum of Natural History where it was "identified" as a rare type of white-tailed deer. The family member was told it was an endangered species, and the museum retained the jacka-lope for over a year before admitting they were wrong.

Sometimes Cabela's receives strange or humorous requests and comments from some of their more eccentric patrons. Dick, Mary and Jim remember some of these and a few stand out in their minds.

They recall one customer who made an unusual request which they could not fulfill. The request was from a young man who wanted to meet one of the models from a catalog. He insisted he was not a pervert and was very religious. He expressed an interest in a long-term relationship. He asked for the model's name and address so he could write her a letter, as if any company in its right mind would give out such information to just anyone who asks for it. My father told me that they obviously did not give the gentleman any information on the model but could only hope he received 100% satisfaction elsewhere.

While we were discussing the different correspondences Cabela's has had with some of its customers, I asked my dad if there were any memorable complaints. He told me about a very negative complaint he thought was quite funny:

"A long time ago when we still sold traps, we heard from a woman whose complaint was very explicit. She thought our catalog was presented well but she had a few problems with the dead ducks painted on the cover. Her biggest complaint though was what she called 'evil animal traps.' She said that we should be ashamed by the pain the traps cause innocent helpless animals. I distinctly remember what she wished on us next. She said she hoped the next time we were out in the woods and pulled down our pants to take a crap that a trap was there and snapped us right in the testicles! There are always rare occasions when we are sometimes unable to fulfill our

100% customer-satisfaction guarantee!"

Once a very creative customer gave the company many praises in the form of a complaint. He went on and on and listed his "gripes" about the catalog, such as product display, the quality of merchandise and the prompt delivery time. He explained how none of the other catalog companies he ordered through did things as well as Cabela's and continued to ask why Cabela's would do such things. He said competitors saved him money because they did not run things as effectively or efficiently and therefore he did not spend money on their merchandise. Cabela's, on the other hand, ran things so well they were costing him money because he would keep ordering from the catalog.

There was still another man who had a complaint about his own wife and wanted Cabela's to assist him with his predicament. It seemed every fall when he and his wife went hunting she would manage to get lost. He had to carry along an extra car battery because his would always run down from honking the horn so she could find her way back to the vehicle. His request was for the company to develop some sort of homing device for his wife. He figured if anyone could come up with such a contrivance it was Cabela's.

Customer emotions in the correspondence has ranged from mad, to grateful, to funny, and sometimes to the just plain wacky. Despite all these differences, Cabela's customers will always share a unique and special love for the outdoors.

Their customers' loyalty is not lost on the Cabelas:

"We at Cabela's, the World's Foremost Outfitter would

like to extend our thanks to all of our customers who have been so loyal throughout the years. Without your patronage our success would not be possible. We are very grateful and will continue to strive to bring you quality service and quality merchandise well into the future."

Gratefully,

DICK CABELA; MARY CABELA; JIM CABELA

10. *Accomplishments Honored*

THE ACCOMPLISHMENTS of the Cabela family are apparent when we consider the hardships they endured and the sacrifices they had to make to create an internationally known corporation from virtually nothing. The determination my dad and Jim have shown has been a trait synonymous with the Cabela family for decades. From the first Cabelas to break away from their own hardships in Czechoslovakia, the determination to strive and succeed in America can only be imagined.

Orphaned at an early age, my great grandfather, James Cabela, sailed to the New World in search of a better life for himself. Most of the Cabelas (pronounced CHA'-BLA in the Old World) who lived before James died from tuberculosis and rarely lived past forty. James broke the devastating strain of tuberculosis in his family when he came to America, and most of his descendants have enjoyed long and healthy lives.

The business sense of Dick and Jim can be traced back to James Cabela, their grandfather, who owned a general store in the small community of Brainard, Nebraska, a town with a population of about 330 today. He believed in excellent customer service and strove to treat the customer beyond what was expected. James passed his philosophy and business sense down to his son, A.C. Cabela, who later owned and operated a small hardware and furniture store in Chappell with his wife Marian. A.C. and Marian in turn passed their knowledge on to their children.

To say that the Cabela brothers are humble is an understatement. They grew up in a small farming community and in a religious family, none of whom believed in tooting their own horns. Religious or not, one has to respect the strong beliefs that have kept the Cabelas a close, loving and generous family. Marian Cabela was, according to one of her granddaughters, as close to a saint as she will ever meet. She had enough love and faith all by herself to keep the Cabela family in God's good grace. Considering how large the Cabela family is, that's a lot of love for one person to give.

My father's determination to succeed started at an early age. The life lessons he had to learn as a boy helped to shape the man he has become today. He rarely talks about it, but one of my father's greatest accomplishments took place when he was a small child infected with polio, a disease which often results in muscular paralysis and in some cases, death. The doctors informed Marian and A.C. that their first child probably would never walk again. His determination pushed him to defeat the crippling disease. Not only did he walk again, but he went on to participate in high school sports.

Marian Cabela used to tell her grandchildren how their father had to battle asthma as a child, as well as polio. She remembers traveling to Omaha during World War II to see an asthma specialist. The hotel they stayed at was only two blocks away, but my dad's asthma was so severe that he could not make it all the way and had to be carried by his mother.

Dad went on to beat the asthma and as a young boy added becoming an Eagle Scout to his list of accomplishments. As a hunter today he often has to traverse the most treacherous terrain in the most extreme conditions for miles upon miles, sometimes never even catching a glimpse of the animal he is hunting, and yet return and do it again the next day.

I once asked about the three Mount Nyala hunts he had been on in Ethiopia. On the first two hunting trips to this high mountainous terrain, my mother and father returned without a Mount Nyala antelope. They finally found success on the third trip.

When I asked him why they kept choosing to go back even though the odds were so strongly against their success, Dad gave a reply which helped me to understand why many of my failures may be the direct result of giving up too easily or too soon:

"First of all, in all of the hunts I have ever been on, I have never once been on an unsuccessful one. Even if you return from a hunt without an animal you do not walk away empty handed. Just think about it. Nine times out of ten, when you go hunting you come back without having made a kill. Some of the most memorable and most successful hunts I have ever been on have been hunts in which I never fired even one shot. Failure and success can only be measured to a certain extent in tangible form and failure can only be determined by him who fails. I believe I have failed in many things in my life, but I choose to find important lessons in every failure. If you believe you have walked away from an experience with nothing, then you have done just that and that is the only way you have failed."

My parents have always led very active lives and have always been more than happy to get involved in causes they believe in. When Dad was still working for his father at the furniture store, he hosted a weekly radio program that focused on local news and politics. Of course, they have always found time for their family and continue to pursue the excitement of the outdoors with eager hearts.

Cabela's has been recognized many times for its accomplishments. My father and my uncle strongly believe the awards and recognition have been attained through a joint effort of everyone involved in the company. They stress that all they have accomplished could never have been possible without the help of others.

At first, it was just Dick and Mary, but they still needed each other to get their improbable business off the ground.

Soon Jim joined the business and the next thing they knew Cabela's Incorporated required thousands of people, with the number still multiplying, to keep it running.

One of the first honors Dick and Jim received for their accomplishments came in 1970, just nine years after they had decided to try their hands in the mail-order industry. They were jointly named the Small Business Administration's "Man of the Year."

Though they enjoyed that certain distinction, Dick reminds us of the most important recognition Cabela's strives for:

"The only real recognition that means all that much in the business world is from your customers. If they do not give you their recognition, then your company will not stay afloat. There are things which you can do to increase your chances for success, but in business the customer ultimately decides your fate."

Dick has represented Cabela's as a member of the Direct Marketing Association (DMA) for many years. The DMA is made up of businesses and individuals whose interests lie within the parameters of direct marketing. In 1987 Dick was elected to the Board of Directors of the DMA, along with five others, including: Carl Von E. Bickert, National Demographics and Lifestyles, Inc; Christie Hefner, Playboy Enterprises; Kenneth Chenault, American Express; and Sheila Martin, Triplex Direct Marketing Corporation.

For several years, Dick was on the board of the Direct Marketing Education Foundation. In 1998 he became chairman elect of the Nebraska Chamber of Commerce and has served on the board of the Wildlife Legislative Fund of America.

In 1994 Dick and Jim were inducted into the Nebraska Business Hall of Fame. Some of the few names also included in this select group are: Warren Buffett, Berkshire Hathaway; Duane Acklie, Crete Carrier Corp; and V.J. Skutt, Mutual of Omaha.

More recently, Dick and Jim received the nation's highest entrepreneur award when they were named the 1999 Ernst and Young Entrepreneurs of the Year in the Retail/Consumer Products category. There were more than 4,000 nominees in twelve different categories, making the award very competitive. Well-known companies such as Best Buy and eBay received awards in their respective categories. One of the aspects of Cabela's which greatly impressed the judges was the humble beginnings the company started with as it grew into a global corporation.

Shortly after they had received this award, Cabela's was recognized by another major business publication. *Fortune* magazine named Cabela's one of the top 100 best companies to work for in the United States. The first time on the list the company debuted at number 84. Less than one year later, the company was listed #410 on the Forbes 500 Top Private Companies list. Their ranking was compiled from estimates of 1999 earnings, as Cabela's does not release financial information. Without divulging any numbers, it is safe to say the estimates were a little low.

Some additional honors bestowed upon Cabela's include: University of Nebraska College of Business Administration Alumni Corporate Leadership Award; Nebraska FBLA Business of the year in 1994; Nebraska Rural Development Commission's top ten rural development initiatives; the U.S. Small Business Administration's Entrepreneurial Success Award; and the *Star-Herald's* Business Citizen of the Century. These are just a few of the forms of special recognition, too many to name, the company has received over the years.

Dick and Jim should feel a small sense of pride in knowing that all the hard work they have put into making Cabela's the success it is today has not gone unnoticed. It has been recognized by their peers, by their state and by the nation, and it has certainly been recognized by all their loyal customers who continue to return time and time again.

When Dad has been asked about the many awards he and Cabela's have received over the years he usually responds in his modest manner:

"It's always nice to be recognized, but all the recognition and all the awards in the world do not mean anything if your customers and employees do not believe in you and are not happy with the way things are going. The bottom line is that our loyal customers and employees have been much more responsible for the recognition we have received than I have personally. Without loyal customers and exceptional employees we would not be where we are today."

Dick and Jim may not agree, but without their hard work, vision, and determination, Cabela's customers and employees would not have such an outstanding company to shop at or work for. They all go hand in hand, and no matter how much the two Cabela brothers try to downplay their role, the significance of their efforts in making Cabela's the success it is today is widely appreciated.

11. | *Generous Nature*

"**B**ACK IN 1982, I had just left Loomis Composites to start building my own machinery for the G. Loomis Company. With only $32.10 left in my bank account, I still had one more piece of machinery to build before I could start manufacturing.

"During this crisis, Dennis Highby called wanting to buy blanks from us to use in the manufacture of Cabela's rods. I explained that at the time I was short one piece of machinery and didn't have the starting funds to be able to supply them with the number of blanks needed, which was a huge amount for my new, start-up company. During the conversation, Dennis asked me how much I would need to get the machine and set up our manufacturing within the time limit. After a little bit of discussion, we came up with a figure of $50,000. Dick and Jim asked for my bank account number, which I gave them and within three days, the $50,000 was in my account. I was able to buy the last piece of machinery and start up production to fill the Cabela's order. Jim and Dick had enough foresight and trust in me, because I didn't even sign any papers for that loan for eight or nine months. I was able to pay it back within two years.

"This was really the beginning of my company, and G. Loomis probably would have been a year or two longer getting started without the help of Jim and Dick Cabela. I think that it's people like those at Cabela's that have helped our industry grow into what it is today. I would personally thank everyone at Cabela's, especially Jim, Dick and Mary, for all the help they gave me at G. Loomis Inc. Thank you."

—Gary Loomis

Some would say it is easy to be generous when you are successful; and they may be right to a certain extent. I've personally known those who are very fortunate and don't have a generous bone in their body. I have also known others who barely have enough to live on and always seem to have something for those they believe need it more.

Anyone who has ever had the pleasure to know the Cabelas knows their generosity. Their success has not made it easier to give, it has just made it easier to give more. Their generosity is a trait which they learned from their parents, and before they were blessed with their success, they gave what they could with the little they had and the time they could spare.

In some ways generosity becomes more difficult with success. It is utterly amazing when you consider the sheer number of people and organizations who want something from those who have attained financial prosperity. Most of them represent legitimate deserving causes, but there are always a few who, for some reason or another, believe those who are financially successful owe them something. These people make it difficult to choose which causes are more deserving.

No matter how much they would like to, it would be quite impossible for the Cabelas to give to every person or organization that wanted something from them. They must pick and choose the causes which they strongly believe in. It is quite a responsibility having the success that Dick and Jim have had.

Cabela's, as a company and the Cabelas personally, have always been willing to help the Make-A-Wish Foundation. For instance, the last few years Cabela's has sponsored a ride in an Iditarod musher's sled for a Make-A-Wish child as part of the Iditarod Idita-Rider program.

Cabela's is a sponsor of the three-time Iditarod Sled Dog Race champion, Jeff King, who gladly takes a Make-A-Wish child in his sled for the Idita-Rider program. In 1998, he took a nine-year old boy with neuroblastoma on the nine-mile portion of the trail the mushers take on their way to the start of the race in Anchorage. When King asked the boy if he would like to ride all the way to Anchorage, he joyfully accepted.

As well as sponsoring the ride for the Make-A-Wish child, Cabela's outfits the child's family with warm clothing and footwear for their stay in the cold climate of Alaska.

Cabela's is often willing to help out causes which are closer to home. Although Dick and Jim have been quick to point out that they believe the City of Sidney has done at least as much, if not more, for Cabela's than Cabela's has done for Sidney, the contributions the company has made to the community are very significant. The economic support the company brings to the area, with all the jobs they supply and outside business they bring in, is an enormous asset.

Dick, Mary and Jim have always believed in loyalty. The Sidney community members have always been loyal to Cabela's and, therefore, Cabela's has remained loyal to Sidney. By merely continuing to do business in the community, Cabela's has proven its loyalty, but they have never been out to prove anything to anyone but themselves. Cabela's does not give back to the community to gain recognition. They give something back because of their loyalty. Cabela's and Sidney have enjoyed what can be called a partnership, and one would just not be the same without the other. Cabela's has no intention of leaving the Sidney area and displayed their loyalty to the town when they built a 120,000-square-foot corporate headquarters.

Cabela's has raised funds for Sidney's Western Nebraska Community College. In addition, they have also been named the Supporter of the Year by the Sidney Jaycees for all they have done to support the local chapter. At one point,

Memorial Health Center, the hospital in Sidney, was raising funds for expansion and remodeling and Cabela's did their part by pledging $500,000 to the effort. That number represented more than a quarter of the overall fundraising goal.

Each year the company stocks the local pond with fish so the children in the area can have a highly accessible place to go fishing. Cabela's has also tagged some of the fish, giving prizes to kids who bring their tags into the showroom. Giving the children a place to catch fish helps to keep some of them from finding less constructive things to do.

The corporation also believes in helping out the great state which helped to shape the minds of the two Cabela brothers. Growing up in rural Nebraska you learn morals and values which are far and away above the norms of today's urban society. Cabela's understands what Nebraska has done for the company and has helped the state to reap some of the rewards from the company's success.

Recently, the state created a new travel marketing partnership hoping to bring more outdoor enthusiasts to the state. The partnership consists of the Nebraska Game and Parks Commission, the Nebraska Division of Travel and Tourism, and, of course, Cabela's, whose stores are the largest tourist attractions in the state.

The state is highly excited about the partnership. Through Cabela's, Nebraska has the opportunity to show the world what it has to offer to the outdoor-loving tourists. Nebraska offers one of the largest varieties of outdoor recreational opportunities in the United States and believes

Cabela's participation in the effort of getting the word out will help to significantly increase the tourism in the state.

Lake McConaughy is Nebraska's largest reservoir and attracts many visitors annually. Naturally, the Nebraska Game and Parks Commission would want to have a facility near this body of water with 35,000 surface acres and the surrounding state recreational area. Cabela's wished to help in any way they could and decided to donate a huge aquarium for freshwater fish native to Nebraska. The aquarium will be used as an educational tool to teach visitors about the diversity of fish that can be found in Nebraska and their importance to the environment.

One of the programs of which Cabela's is extremely proud to be a sponsor is "Hooked on Fishing, Not on Drugs," considered one of the most effective tools for keeping kids away from drugs. The programs were started by the Future Fishermen Foundation and are used across the United States. They consist of teaching children about the importance of fishing and how to catch fish. The programs are normally put on by local organizations and sponsored by local and national organizations. Along with many other organizations and companies, Cabela's is proud to call itself one of the companies helping to keep kids away from drugs.

Dick, Mary and Jim have always believed they as individuals and as officers of a corporation have a responsibility to help conserve the wildlife populations we enjoy today because of the foresight of hunters, anglers and conservationists who came before us. As individuals, as well as a corporation, they give as much as possible to deserving conservation and wildlife groups such as the Wildlife Heritage Alliance, Ohioans for Wildlife Conservation, Safari Club International and Wildlife Legislative Fund of America, where Dick serves on the board.

Cabela's recently received the Director's Corporate Wildlife Stewardship Award from the U.S. Fish and Wildlife Service. Cabela's contributed nearly $50,000 worth of equipment to help combat poaching in Africa and special agents of the U.S. Fish and Wildlife Service delivered the gear to the Lusaka Task Force, a coalition of nine African nations which enforce wildlife laws.

Cabela's introduced a Wildlife Conservation Calendar in 1999. The company uses the calendar to honor wildlife conservation organizations for all they have done and continue to do to ensure that we continue to have healthy wildlife populations. Cabela's also uses the calendar to urge others to join these conservation groups in their efforts to conserve our wildlife. Some of the conservation groups featured in the calendar include: Wildlife Forever, Quail Unlimited, Ruffed Grouse Society, National Wild Turkey Federation, Trout Unlimited, Foundation for North American Wild Sheep, Safari Club International, Pope and Young Club, Rocky Mountain Elk Foundation, Ducks Unlimited, Whitetails Unlimited, Pheasants Forever, Boone and Crockett Club, Delta Waterfowl, Hunters Alliance, Orion, and Wildlife Legislative Fund of America.

These and other true conservation groups use the support of their members to conserve wildlife, unlike some anti-hunting and anti-fishing groups who use their funds to push their political agenda, doing nothing to benefit and conserve wildlife.

Without groups such as these and the individuals and organizations who donate their time and money, we would not be blessed with the ability to enjoy the great wildlife the earth's vast natural world holds. Whether or not you hunt and fish, these organizations, the people who support them, and hunters and anglers all over the world, deserve our thanks for all they have done to ensure that wild places will always have a home on earth.

Besides merely giving through Cabela's, Dick and Mary and Jim give to these and other organizations with their personal income. With Dick, Mary, and Jim all coming from strong Catholic backgrounds, they also give emphatically to a number of churches, especially those they visit often when at home or traveling.

My parents come from humble backgrounds and know what it means to struggle. Therefore, it is not surprising to discover that a favorite charity of theirs is Food for the Poor.

Hollywood is sometimes guilty of identifying success with greed, even though many associated with film making are quite well-off themselves. If success truly sprang from greed, why is it that when the economy grows and more people become successful, charitable donations grow as well? I know far more financially successful people of generous natures than the greedy, evil mongrels often portrayed in the entertainment industry.

Dick knew at an early age that success did not come easily and that most who have achieved it have worked very hard to do so. Dick says it is how we achieve that success and what we do with it that gives us the respect of others. The Cabelas have earned this respect, and anyone who has ever had the pleasure to know them has given it to them.

12. *Expanding Horizons*

A S CABELA'S HAS GROWN they have ventured into new areas of business and moved existing portions of the company to new locations. Cabela's has become much larger than my dad had ever expected. When he first began selling his hand-tied flies he had no idea that he would eventually need three separate locations just to take phone orders. He had no way of knowing he would need a better distribution system than loading orders into the old green van and dropping them off at the Chappell post office.

The distribution system in Sidney continues to work exceptionally, but Cabela's ran into that same old problem once again—space. As a remedy, Cabela's built two 300,000-square-foot buildings in Prairie du Chien,

Wisconsin. Essentially, the same distribution system is used as that which has been refined in Sidney. However, the Prairie Du Chien location has been given the responsibility of shipping all shoes and other clothing, as well as other items, from its location.

The way Cabela's distributes its merchandise has undergone transformation after transformation and, in all likelihood, will continue to be refined as technology continues to advance and as the company continues to learn. The outstanding growth of Cabela's has forced Dick and Jim to expand their operations to new locations. With every expansion and new location, more jobs are created and Cabela's is better prepared to serve their customers.

The company's growth and expansion not only benefit the corporation itself, but many others as well. Local economies are uplifted, jobs are created for thousands of individuals, and those who love the outdoors are given better service and better opportunity to purchase their ever important outdoor equipment.

Distribution isn't the only area of the company where growth has been reason for a move to a new location. The telemarketing department has also enjoyed continuous expansion. Having had no plans for taking orders by phone, Cabela's has gone from one phone to hundreds of phones for taking orders, in three separate cities in Nebraska. The three cities include Grand Island, North Platte, and Kearney, each boasting more than 170 employees, most of whom work on the phones.

The returns department has also expanded and moved to a new location. All returns are now sent to Oshkosh, Nebraska. The merchandise is evaluated and any damaged goods are sent to the Bargain Cave in one of the retail locations. If an item was never used and is returned for a reason such as being the wrong size, it is returned to the regular stock. The employees in the returns department would take it very personally if an item damaged or with any wear made its way back into the regular stock.

Dad and Jim have expanded Cabela's horizons into other arenas as well. For instance, they had never intended to be in the restaurant business, yet the restaurants in the catalog showrooms have become favorite eating places for some of the local residents and consumers. Very little money is made by these restaurants, but Dick and Jim believe the convenience for their retail customers, many of whom are traveling, makes the retail restaurants essential regardless of the dollar amount they bring in.

Dick and Jim never dreamed their last name would be associated with a travel agency, and yet Cabela's Outdoor Adventures is one of the most well respected agencies when it comes to booking hunting and fishing trips for the adventurous traveler. Whenever I plan a trip to a new destination I always go through Outdoor Adventures because I know I can trust the judgment of these experts of outdoor travel. Whether you want to hunt elk in Montana, catch trophy king salmon in Alaska, or experience the untamed land of Africa on a Safari, Cabela's Outdoor Adventures can send you to the best places. Many of the employees have visited these loca-tions and therefore have given Cabela's Outdoor Adventures first-hand information.

Although Cabela's now owns a travel agency, Dick and Jim have not broken the rule they were taught with their doomed housewares catalog—stick with what you know. By specializing in hunting and fishing expeditions, Cabela's Outdoor Adventures has not strayed far from that painful rule.

Cabela's Outdoor Adventures will book trips anywhere a client wishes to go, but they specialize in outdoor travel plans like hunting and fishing trips. By focusing their efforts in this area, agents can arrange enjoyable hunts and fishing trips and provide Cabela's customers with the best possible service.

Cabela's Outdoor Adventures is a full-service travel agency and books almost every type of trip. However, the name Cabela's has become synonymous with hunting, fishing, and the outdoors. Millions of customers trust the Cabela name when it comes to outfitting themselves for outdoor excursions. In addition, many outdoor enthusiasts have learned to trust the Cabela name for planning extended trips, which may take them fishing, camping or even on a honey-moon in Africa.

To expand their horizons even further, Dick and Jim invested company funds in another venture called Sportsman's Quest. Sportsman's Quest traveled the country to conduct a variety of events such as fishing tournaments, sporting-clays tournaments, archery tournaments, black powder competi-tions and sporting-dog trials.

Sportsman's Quest is also the host of a television and radio show of the same name. The TV program is currently aired on ESPN and offers the viewer a look into the world of the outdoor conservationists who call themselves hunters and anglers. The cameras follow celebrities such as former Dallas Cowboy Jay Novacek around the world on hunting and fishing expeditions, and allow the viewers to see some of the highlights of the various events.

During the show, the viewer can witness the successes of hunters and anglers in the field or on the water. I refrain from using the word *failures* with *successes* because for a hunter or an angler, having the chance to hunt or fish is always a success.

This is not to say every show features hunters or anglers harvesting their quarry. If a hunter or angler succeeded every time, there would be no challenge to pull them back out into the wilderness. A statement nearly every hunter or angler would agree with is that the more difficult the hunt, the more memorable and enjoyable the hunt. Some of the greatest hunts demand hours, days, weeks, and sometimes years of hard work without ever harvesting an animal. It truly is the journey which is most important.

There was one particular Sportsman's Quest episode where the host and another man were bow hunting in south-central Nebraska. The camera focused on a large number of beautiful deer. The hunters and the deer could be seen together in the same frame, but the animals managed to stay just out of bow range. As the episode came to a close, both hunters walked away from the field with wide genuine grins from another unique and wonderful day in the wild. No animal was harvested and yet neither hunter showed an ounce of disappointment.

Most recently, Cabela's partnered with Vulcan Publishing to create a new magazine dedicated to a hunting, fishing and camping readership. The new top quality outdoor periodical gives Cabela's another method to help educate and entertain sportsmen and women across the country. *Outfitter Journal* offers its readers all the outdoor news, tips and stories they would expect from a magazine by the World's Foremost Outfitter.

A major technological change that has found its way to Cabela's is the mass market opportunities of the Internet. Cabelas.com is a relatively young website, but then so are the majority of websites. Launched in October of 1998, Cabelas.com has exceeded every projection for growth accounting for more than five percent of the company's business. In addition to the catalogs and the retail stores, Cabela's customers now have another source to purchase their outdoor wares—Cabela's Online Store. Online customers can browse through more than 5,200 pages of outdoor products, and once they find a product they wish to purchase, they can feel safe ordering through Cabela's secure site. Unlike many dot-coms, who may never see a profit, Cabelas.com became highly profitable immediately.

The Cabelas.com website also allows the customer to apply for a No Fee Cabela's CLUB Visa, read articles about the outdoors, order catalogs, read about the retail stores, communicate with customer-service representatives and link up with other outdoor websites. With the number of people using the internet rising every day, the Cabela's Online Store is sure to continue to experience the same kind of steady growth the rest of the company has seen.

The Cabela's Credit Card Club was introduced in 1995. The Visa card is especially valuable to Cabela's customers who use it. For each dollar spent the card holder receives one Cabela's point. In addition, for each dollar spent on the card at Cabela's, the holder receives double Cabela's points.

As these points accumulate they can be redeemed to purchase Cabela's merchandise. The more the customer uses the card, especially at Cabela's, the more points one acquires. The more points acquired, the more outdoor equipment from Cabela's the customer can purchase. I even find myself using my credit card for almost everything just so I can accumulate more Cabela's points to help pay for the new equipment my wife says I do not need.

Cabela's ventured into the taxidermy industry when the company acquired Van Dykes. Van Dykes has been a leader in the taxidermy field for over fifty years and is dedicated to offering quality taxidermy supplies to taxidermists everywhere. As a catalog company it is a perfect match for Cabela's. The Van Dykes Taxidermy Catalog is filled with more than 200 pages of supplies for both the expert taxidermist and the aspiring novice.

Cabela's is known best for its quality-filled catalog and excellent customer service. However, Dick and Jim have created a company which is much more than that. Cabela's expansion is extraordinary no matter how we look at it. Dick and Jim have always looked to the horizon and always strive to take Cabela's to the next step. The first expansions were made because of a necessity for space. Continued growth today creates more need for expansion into other locations. All expansion has not, however, arisen because of necessity from growth. Sometimes, the brothers are approached with new opportunities and after careful research and planning, just like to try new things.

Dick and Jim, although satisfied with all they have accomplished, cannot be satisfied with the supposition that there is nothing left to accomplish. They created Cabela's with their own sweat and ingenuity and turned the company into the World's Foremost Outfitter because they refuse to be short-sighted and will always look beyond the next horizon.

13. The Juggling Act

"I will always remember the family atmosphere that Jim, Dick and Mary created within the company and how their personal values shined through Cabela's. Dick never goes anywhere without Mary and their names are always said in unison. Jim, although a bachelor, has strong family values and it is evident in the way they support their employees. It is a great environment in which to raise a family."

—Pat Snyder
Director of Merchandising—
Clothing

THE RESPONSIBILITIES AND TIME requirements of raising a family are extremely demanding, for sure. Throw in starting a business from scratch and any personal free time can be tossed out the window.

For my dad there never seemed to be enough time for either one of these endeavors. Both required a substantial amount of commitment. When he was at work, he often felt he should be at home, and when he was at home, he often felt he should be working on his business. On the one hand, he needed to provide for his growing family; on the other, he knew how important it was that his family receive the attention they desired.

My father came from a family in which his father had to make enough time for the furniture store as well as his wife and children. A.C. Cabela provided Dad with an excellent example of how to raise a family and run a business at the same time.

As to his own childhood, Dad was not dealt a royal flush, although you would never hear any complaints from him. I have rarely heard him speak of his early years, but what he recalls is filled with joy and wonder, not sickness or struggle.

There were no health problems that could keep Dad from the outdoor world. His was a spirit that could not be contained within the confines of walls. He longed to spend as much time as possible in the wild. Even when he was extremely sick and could hardly move, his mother had to force him to stay in bed, and kept a constant watch on him in case he tried to sneak out the back door.

Dick and Jim both could have been content with merely observing the wild wonders they explored, but their natural instincts called on them to become a part of their environment. The lure of the hunt could not easily be suppressed in boys who grew up witnessing the brutal but aesthetic dance of life and death. They were aware at an early age that life was completely impossible without death. Rather than reject this unchangeable truth they chose to follow their instincts and become an honest part of the circle of life.

The time the two boys spent in secluded wild places of the Nebraska panhandle greatly helped to shape the men they have become. Their love for the wilderness has never wavered and their instincts are as strong as ever, pulling them back to nature. They have always known the important role anglers and hunters, such as their customers and themselves, play in the natural world.

This call to the wild along with strong family values made Dad a perfect candidate for the Boy Scouts of America. He joined at an early age and stuck with it until finally becoming an Eagle Scout.

Dick still believes that the Boy Scouts were an important part of his childhood years:

"Although the love and support of my parents and the values they taught me were the biggest influence in my life, the time I spent outside and with the Boy Scouts was also important. In my youth, the Boy Scouts gave me a sense of purpose and responsibility early on. They helped to give me goals to strive for and challenged me to reach them. I still have goals which I try to reach and the Boy Scouts of America taught me how important it was to have aims and to stick with them, never giving up. Those lessons I learned have stayed with me and have helped me to continue reaching for my goals."

Many things help to shape a person's life, of course. Some more important than others. For my father, the most influential parts of his childhood included his family, nature, belonging to organizations like the Boy Scouts and sports teams, and most important, God. God has always been an unalterable part of the Cabela family life.

Before he retired, Mark Wieser ran the retail division and remembers the Cabelas always finding time for the more important things in life:

"I've hunted elk and turkey with Jim on several occasions and you can't find a better hunting partner, both in the field and at camp. One of the things I truly admire most about Jim, Dick and Mary is the fact that as busy and hectic as their lives are, they always have time to practice their faith and realize who is really running the world."

To me, faith is an important part of life. Whether the faith is in God or in another person or even in oneself, we all have faith in something at one time or another. Dick Cabela's faith in God is his own and he believes it has given him strength to have faith in others and, more important, in himself:

"I could not understand a life without God. To me, a life without the Lord would be meaningless. God has always been a part of my life and I believe I am a much better person as a result."

Every aspect of the Cabelas' lives has included their faith and every time they venture into the wild and untouched places of the world that faith is strengthened. They believe that among all the beautiful things human hands have made, none will ever compare to God's magnificent and pure creations.

As time has passed, the most influential aspects of Dick's life remain unchanged. He was brought up with strong family values, and thus it is not surprising he raised a family of his own. His wife, Mary, shared his faith and love of family life, prompting them eventually to have nine children of their own. Their children have all grown and chosen their individual paths, but none of us can ever question the love of our parents and we know that family in all its forms should always be cherished.

Raising a family has to be one of the more difficult tasks a person can undertake. It is also one of the most rewarding. The struggles involved are never-ending and require constant attention, but, the love and joy of a family is also forever and cannot be matched.

Families are like the stripes on a zebra—no two are the same. Despite all the books teaching the "right way" to raise children, all parents must make their own mistakes and do the best they can. Our parents know they were not experts when they started having children, but the desire for a family was strong for both of them.

Dick also knows just how difficult building a business from essentially nothing can be. He is proud of his accomplishments, but remembers more challenging times:

"Other than the trials of polio as a child, raising children was probably one of the most challenging and demanding parts of my life. We made some mistakes, but what parent hasn't? One of the most difficult, yet joyful experiences a person can expect is having a child . . . or nine."

Dick and Mary reared four girls and five boys, not a simple task. Throw in creating a corporate family and it is amazing they had enough time for sleep. Quality time management was extremely important, especially during the first years of business when Dad worked in the furniture store and could spend time on his own company only after working hours.

During that first couple of years, Dad did not get to spend as much time with his children as he would have liked. The little time he did have with us was very special to him and he made it count.

Many of Dick's most memorable days are those he spent with his family:

"We always made it a point to take a least one family trip each year and many years two. Like most family vacations ours always had their fair share of mishaps. The car would break down, one of the kids would get sick, or even lost. I don't think we ever took a family trip which does not hold wonderful memories for us all."

The challenges of raising a family, as any parent knows, are insistent. Nurturing an idea and following through by creating something like a business with hard work and perseverance, is also a demanding choice. Combine two such efforts as Dick and Mary Cabela have done, and the demands are truly never ending.

Like most parents who have to juggle their time between providing for their families and playing with their families, Dad found it nearly impossible to fit everything in. He learned to manage his time and always seemed to be able be there for the important events that his family and his business needed him for.

The Cabelas have spent a lifetime raising two families, one in their home and one in their business. They gave both plenty of attention, care, and love. Things did not always go as planned, but they have no regrets and can rest easy knowing they did the best they could with both families. They had a lot of help and support along the way, especially from their personal family, which they greatly appreciated and certainly needed. By any standard they did a good job with both families and can believe their best was far beyond adequate.

14. Essential Tackle for a Successful Catalog Company

DICK CABELA UNDERSTANDS ALL TOO WELL what it takes to create and build a catalog company. His sweat and tears laid the foundation to the company we have grown to trust when it comes to acquiring gear and advice for our outdoor excursions. Dick has compiled for us a short list of some of the points he feels are important in the catalog and direct-marketing industry. Reading this list in no way will completely prepare us to begin our own catalog companies, but they are solid and fundamental guidelines which, in most instances, should be followed.

CUSTOMER SERVICE. Customer service is definitely the backbone of our business. A backbone that bends but won't break. Superior service gives you an edge keeping your customers. Having a superior product is also very important but without the superior service to back it up your customers will go someplace else, where they can get the same product and that little something extra. The best way to keep your customers coming back and, just as important, referring their acquaintances to you, is to provide them with the extraordinary customer service they desire.

TESTING. One of the most important words in direct marketing is a four-letter word: "test." You must test each new idea before a complete rollout. Our scale is bigger than it was when we almost went under with that disastrous housewares catalog. We learned a painful lesson that year. Today, I would never dream of doing an all-out mailing without doing some extensive testing beforehand. This rule is even more important as your company grows. In the beginning years risks were a necessity if we were going to survive and grow. Some of those risks very nearly put us out of business. We still take risks today. In fact, every time we release a new catalog or open a new retail facility there is always great risk involved. The risks we take today are quite calculated and the calculation comes from testing each of our ideas before we put them into full swing.

TIME. I cannot stress enough the amount of time a venture such as this takes. Do not get the wrong impression about the commitment and time we put into this, especially in the beginning years. Even though I held a full-time job, countless hours were spent making this work. Looking back, the time we spent planning and working and planning and working is astonishing. The truth of the matter is, I had two full-time jobs which together consisted of many sixteen-hour days. Even after I no longer worked in the Chappell furniture store, sixteen-hour days were not uncommon. This cannot be done as a hobby. It takes planning, commitment and a ton of hard work. Although the work is hard, painstakingly long and sometimes seems as if it may all be leading nowhere, the satisfaction of creating something and watching it grow is well worth the time.

DISTINCTIVE POSITIONING. There are thousands and thousands of catalogs out there today vying for a piece of the consumers' business. Believe me, I found out the hard way that you need to have a niche; Cabela's customers have never wanted to see their outdoor catalogs filled with housewares. When we first started, outdoor-gear catalogs were not as common as they are today. We found a market which was relatively unexplored and after a couple of wrong turns we dedicated ourselves to the outdoor-gear industry with no regrets. Today, creating a new catalog which is distinctive is imperative. In today's direct marketing industry a "me too" approach will make success extremely difficult. By the way, a hunting-and-fishing catalog has already been done. However, if a housewares catalog is your cup of tea, I will have no complaints.

ANALYSIS. Direct marketing has evolved into a science of its own. Cost-effectiveness is achieved best by knowing who your customers are. Successful direct marketing requires that we spend hours of each day pouring over tedious reports. Although the reports are tedious and sometimes seem never ending, they become an integral part of any catalog business. It is important for us to know in which direction the consumer is heading so we can be better prepared to serve them. In-house reports, as well as out-of-house reports must be studied to determine their importance and what, if any, action should be taken. The learning process is never ending in all walks of life. Business is no different. The business world changes continuously, and without a continuous education, all too often the decisions made from our analysis may very well be the wrong ones. Although analysis and continued education may not guarantee success they will help keep you in the right direction.

FLEXIBILITY. If you wish to succeed you must become accustomed to a word that all too many businesses fail to adhere to: "change." To change requires flexibility. Do not get caught up into a "what's good today is good tomorrow" mentality. In other words, swim upstream finding your own niche in the marketplace. Too many thriving young businesses get caught in the current and by the time they discover they have drifted downstream, the current is too strong and it is impossible to find their way back upstream. I cannot stress nearly enough the ability to be flexible. However, there is also such a thing as too much flexibility. The way we at Cabela's have done things has changed dramatically over the years, but our philosophy and aim have remained the same. Besides a few wrong turns, we have been dedicated to supplying the outdoor enthusiast with quality equipment and service. Quality merchandise, superb customer service, and the ability to be flexible will help you keep a steady pace upstream for the long term.

EXCEED YOUR CUSTOMERS' EXPECTATIONS. This goes back to the idea of excellent customer service, but it also goes beyond that. Consumers have grown to expect quality customer service, and to be successful you must reach beyond those expectations. This includes giving your customers that extra something. What that extra something is depends on what it is you are trying to sell. It can be something as simple as a free gift or a friendly greeting. When you add that friendly smile or voice to a 100%-satisfaction guarantee, customers feel reassured that, even if they later decide they purchased the wrong item, they can return it virtually hassle free. Exceeding your customers' expectations includes offering them new products as well as the tried-and-true. Make sure to keep ahead of the game and offer them before reports come out showing consumer trends, because by then you are already too late. Remember, consumers always have expectations about what you should be offering and how they should be treated. The successful entrepreneur will always be looking for ways to exceed those expectations.

CONTROLLED GROWTH. No matter how much we wish it were true, overnight success in this business is not in the cards. Success requires hard work, determination, and definitely time. Many entrepreneurs find themselves on the road to success and then over-extend their capabilities. Don't let this happen to you. There can be too much of a good thing. Once you have had a taste of how rewarding success can be, it is easy to want more. That's okay, just don't go after it too fast. It took us nearly four decades of steady, controlled growth to get to where we are today. We have been very successful for many years and have watched many companies, some of them larger and some smaller than ours, try to take too big a piece of the pie too quickly. All too often, if we eat too much too quickly, the results can be disastrous. If you look for the long term growth and solutions you can avoid becoming a victim of your own success.

CUSTOMER DATABASE. In direct marketing, your customer database is one of your most important pieces of information. Some companies rent lists from other companies and that's fine, but rented lists will never compare to a database you have built from actual customers. When we started, there was no such thing as renting lists and our first customer database consisted of one name. That list has grown significantly over the years and continues to grow as new customers discover our catalog. You will find the database you have built for yourself will be on target more often than the rented lists. A lot of effort goes into the maintenance of your customer files and information. Record at least the name and address of every customer, because those who have purchased from you or used your services once are likely to do so again. You would be lucky to hit one out of a thousand, randomly taking names from a telephone book. The way in which you begin to build your own list is entirely up to you. Be original; a small ad and the power from word of mouth can do amazing things for you.

SURROUND YOURSELF WITH TOP-NOTCH PEOPLE. The quality of the people who work for you will have a huge impact on the success of any venture. A company is only as good as the people who run it, and by the people who run it I mean employees at all levels. Make sure to treat all of your employees not only fairly, but well. They treat you well by making your company work and in turn deserve the respect and devotion of their employers. The two most important groups of people at any place of business should always be their customers and their employees. It helps to have people selling your products who use them and truly believe in their quality. It may take a little more to hire a high-quality work force and to treat them well, but the benefits far outweigh the costs.

HONESTY. For any longevity in this or any industry you must be honest with your customers, your employees, and yourself. Your customers will eventually find out if you are not on the level and will make any success you have had very short-lived. Your employees will lose all respect for an untruthful employer and if they do not quit, they surely will not put their hearts into their work. If you lie to yourself, then it doesn't matter what your customers or employees think of you, because you will have a hard time thinking too much of yourself. I have kept a poem titled "The Guy In The Glass" on the back of my business card for years which I believe exemplifies this point. I have tried to live my life with honor and honesty and hope I have taught my children to do the same.

MONEY. Finally, the big "M" word. Things are a little different today than they were when we started in 1961. The kitchen table has become much more expensive at the turn of the century. Number one and two on this list of expenses are paper and postage. I do not wish these last requirements to discourage anyone from striving to reach their goals. Even though the kitchen table has become more expensive, the ways in which to acquire working capital have also become more accessible. There are also many ways to cut costs until you can get on your feet. One is to do all the work yourself, as we did in the beginning. We spent all day working our regular jobs, and all night plus the weekends working on the business and we did not hire any employees until it was absolutely necessary. Reaching your goals may not be easy, but it shouldn't be. The harder the goal is to reach, the sweeter it is once attained.

Few people have been more successful than Dick and Jim Cabela in the direct-marketing catalog industry. Their advice should at least be considered if you dream of success in this arena. Many of these suggestions can be valuable in any business. Dick and Jim do not claim to have all the answers, but they know what has worked for them and by following these few guidelines, one will at least be headed in the right direction.

15. | *What It All Means*

WHAT IS TAKEN AWAY FROM THIS BOOK will vary with each individual, but there is a lesson to be learned here which the Cabelas hope has not been overlooked. If the readers of this book take only one thing from it, let it be that the American Dream is still alive. You would never convince Dick, Mary, or Jim that the American Dream is a thing of the past. They also know that the American Dream is much bigger than achieving financial success. In its purest form the American Dream is nothing less than freedom itself.

Dick, Mary and Jim took a simple idea and fulfilled their dreams. They believed in themselves and in each other, strengthening their chances for success. They pushed and supported each other to work hard and not to give up.

I cannot recall a time in which they gave up easily, or sometimes even willingly. That is not to say they have always accomplished everything they have set out to do. But, they have always been determined to finish what they started. This attitude tends to rub off on others and many who have been a part of Cabela's over the years have achieved great success out of their own determination.

Pat Snyder recognizes Dick, Mary and Jim's desire for everyone, especially their family and employees, to strive for their dreams:

"Often over the course of an evening meal Dick, Jim and their father would reflect on the amazing growth of Cabela's. Jim, always quiet and methodical, would sit and listen, seldom speaking. But, when he did speak, everyone at the table was all ears; his comments were always well thought out and profound.

"One evening, Dick proudly stated to his father, 'Dad, this is the American Dream.' This statement still rings in my ears today because it is the backbone of Dick, Mary and Jim's philosophy towards their employees. They sincerely want each and every one of them to share the American Dream with them. The company's reward from this is an unparalleled level of motivation and dedication from Cabela's employees."

From a small ad in a Wyoming newspaper which generated only a single order, the Cabelas refused to give up and created a company with over sixty million customers around the world. They went from receiving twenty-five pennies taped to a piece of cardboard to receiving thousands of credit-card orders over the phones every day. They went from offering one set of hand-tied flies in 1961 to offering more than 90,000 products at the end of the millennium. And they went from doing all work themselves to over 6100 employees. Through it all they have never forgotten how it started. They still live in Sidney, Nebraska, less than thirty miles from Chappell, the very town in which Dick and Jim grew up hunting rabbits in the back yard.

One important lesson they have learned along the way is relevant in all walks of life. They have found that where you are at is not as important as how you got there. The rewards are only a product of the process, and the more laborious the process the more substantial the rewards.

The Cabelas have devoted most of their lives to "The World's Foremost Outfitter." As Dick, Mary, and Jim have grown, they feel they have worked for and achieved the means to follow their God-given right to pursue adventures in the outdoors. They achieved these means because of their love for the outdoors and a belief that they themselves play an important role in the circle of life.

Dick Cabela knows how important it is to pursue your dreams and your passions in life:

"I do not know if anyone can actually learn anything from our lives, but I hope they will follow their dreams, as we have, and strive to live life to the fullest. To follow your dreams is a phrase we all too often use and would like to do, but somehow never seem to find the time. Sometimes we lack the courage to try. If we never try, we will never know. Dreams rarely come true by themselves. We have to work hard and commit ourselves to sticking with it. I would like to believe, by looking at Cabela's, others will choose to reach for their goals and look beyond the next day to what they wish to become."

Dick and Jim Cabela followed their dreams and pursued their passions. They used their knowledge of fishing and hunting to bring the customer better-quality merchandise. They also used the knowledge passed on by their parents to provide excellent customer service. Their achievements are a result of many different factors, but first and foremost is their belief that dreams are attainable.

Anyone who has ever met Dick or Jim knows they are humble men of few words. To get them to talk about themselves and their accomplishments is quite a task. On the other hand, they can often be heard praising others. Dick rarely shows pride in himself, but when it comes to his family he beams with pride. To hear him speak of his children you would think they were all destined to be president.

Dick and Jim have often been asked how they managed to do it. Their answers are always in praise of others. Usually, they give most, if not all, the credit to employees, or associates as they are referred to in the company. The trust they give those associates has only paid them greater rewards, and they would be the first to confirm this.

Most people enjoy their privacy and do not particularly enjoy others prying into their lives. In our society, a person's private life is far too often flashed throughout the media. The

Cabelas have sometimes been charged with being extremely secretive when it comes to company figures. For the most part, this is the truth. The reason is simply that interviews and information have too often been distorted and inaccurate. The Cabelas have become more reticent over the years, partly as a result of bad experiences and partly just because they enjoy their privacy.

Here is Dick Cabela's own account of how Cabela's grew from the kitchen table to the "World's Foremost Outfitter":

"The history of Cabela's is a direct-marketing success story, and the company is now known in virtually every country in the world. We started with a handful of dollars and a dream. It is a true story of two brothers who loved to go fishing and hunting as children. Now, Jim and I are slightly older brothers who still love to go fishing and hunting and have turned that passion into a business. I was blessed with a loving wife who shares that passion. Mary has been a strong partner and influence in the creation of an international company started at the kitchen table, eventually to become known as 'The World's Foremost Outfitter'."

Index

and the Cabela brothers, 75-
76
in Mexico, 92-94
in Panama, 97
for salmon, 101-102
for walleye, 101-102
flyers (*see* catalog)
Food for the Poor, 192
Football Hall of Fame, 131
Fortune magazine's top 100, 182
Foundation for North American
Wild Sheep, 191
Fuson, Jack, 36, 58
Future Fishermen Foundation,
190

Garcia Corporation, 24
generosity, and the Cabela
family, 186-192
golf equipment, addition to
Cabela's line, 18, 23, 30, 41
Grant, Bud, 131
growth, 33-34, 53-59, 60-62, 68-
73, 84, 110-111, 117-118, 120-
138, 140-145
and movement, 195-199, 196-
202
summary, 222-223, 225
survey of, 114-118
without cannibalization, 112-
113, 131
guarantees, 18, 19-20, 26, 40,
115-116, 170
"Guy in the Glass (The)" 159-
160, 218

Hamby, Mike, 137
Harvey, Carolyn, 92-94

High Plains Cache restaurant,
122, 125
Highby, Dennis, 98-99, 135,
185-186
honesty, 217-218
"Hooked on Fishing, Not on
Drugs," 190
housewares, 26-27, 28-29
Hunters Alliance, 191
hunting and fishing
big game, 84
concentration on supplies, 35,
43-44
Dick's early love of fishing, 5
for elk, 94, 101
for geese, 104-106
meaning of, 199
in Nebraska, 79
pheasant, 99-100
its purpose, 80

Iditarod, 131, 144
Iditarod Idita-Rider program,
187-188
Sled Dog Race, 187
Idol, Dick, 128, 131
inflation, 18, 32
integrity, and success, 40
Internet, the
and marketing, 200-202
and sales, 117
inventory
adding categories, 18, 23, 25,
26-27, 29-30, 35
building, 10, 15, 18, 20, 24, 25
discontinuance of items, 27,
41
growth, 71